# NOW
# WHAT?

★ ★ ★

# NOW WHAT?

★ ★ ★

HOW NORTH CAROLINA

CAN BLAZE A PROGRESSIVE

PATH FORWARD

★ ★ ★

Gene Nichol

— BLAIR —

Printed in the United States of America
Cover design by Ashton Smith
Interior design by April Leidig

Blair is an imprint of Carolina Wren Press.

*The mission of Blair/Carolina Wren Press is to seek out, nurture,
and promote literary work by new and underrepresented writers.*

We gratefully acknowledge the ongoing support of
general operations by the Durham Arts Council's United Arts Fund
and the North Carolina Arts Council.

North
Carolina
Arts
Council
*Fifty years
of leadership*

**DURHAM**
ARTS COUNCIL

ISBN 9781958888674 paperback
ISBN 9781958888742 ebook

Library of Congress Control Number: 2025944886

*For my girls:*

*Glenn, Jesse, Jenny, Soren, Annabelle, and Evangeline*

# CONTENTS

# NOW WHAT?

★ ★ ★

★ ★ ★

## CHAPTER ONE

# Introduction

## A Democratic North Carolina

These are, no doubt, challenging times for friends, or believing heirs, of constitutional democracy—both nationally and in the state I love, North Carolina. Democracy is still, surprisingly, under siege, sometimes even violently. Political leaders assert and accumulate illegitimate, entrenched powers forbidden by an ancient constitutional structure—thus threatening foundational rights of equal political participation and an essential dedication to the consent of the governed. Government authority is used to make dissent costly or even dangerous. Civil rights guarantees that were long thought secured are consistently targeted in favor of an assumed white Christian primacy. Pluralistic democracy is thought to be increasingly unacceptable if it diminishes a permanent tribal ascendancy. Marginalized communities suffer even greater degradations. Low-income citizens are continually cast aside in what is already the most economically unequal nation in human history. In Washington, DC, and in state capitals across the country, restrictions on democracy and liberty that would have been summarily invalidated a half-century ago are now embraced. We move decidedly, month after month, farther away from Abraham Lincoln's defining dedication to government of, by, and for (all) the people.

This book is an odd one. It explores an American war on democracy and constitutional governance, and yet it is not about Donald Trump. He hangs over the discussions, of course, as well as everything else in our national life. And he appears here indirectly on occasion. But this short effort is about the distinct, though related, war on constitutional democracy in one particular and profoundly southern state: North Carolina. What that war is, what it threatens to become, and, most importantly, what progressive and committed Tar Heels can do to defeat it. And, I'll suggest, as a lot of people here already understand, that we face what Dr. King deemed a "fierce urgency" to defeat it now. This year. This cycle. This season. Time, in North Carolina, is not democracy's friend.

I suppose it is already implicit that I believe the war on democracy in the Tar Heel State is somehow different, divergent, at variance with the horrors we presently witness on the national stage. So let me be explicit about that. I'm convinced our antidemocratic crusade, or regime, is distinct in character, in strategy, and in aesthetic from much of Trumpism. Its façade is more appealing, less overtly boorish and threatening, and more accepted and, seemingly, acceptable. It is less visibly steeped in hatred and cruelty—though its exclusions tend to match precisely those of its forebears. As I explain in the next chapter, it is more rooted in power—and in the distorting structures of power it has created, implemented, and revealed—than in the overt and public embrace of malevolence. North Carolina's sedition work is both superficially better and operationally worse than its national counterpart. It is more successfully costumed and packaged, wrapped in lapel flags and chamber of commerce memberships, in evangelical pieties and protestations of so-called law and order, than its brutal national cousin. Yet its snares may well prove more strategic, more enduring, and even more challenging to escape than a (federal) political rubric that is more directly and overtly premised in animosity.

But if North Carolina Republicans have developed powerful and unrelenting mechanisms to cheat their way into and entrench themselves in power, even still, there is potent reason for optimism among Tar Heel progressives. And this book dwells, principally, on those avenues of hope. North Carolina is not a ruby-red counterpart of most of its southern, former Confederate kin. Believers in pluralist democracy, through a foundational frame of constitutional liberty, can have reason for confidence in North Carolina. And this effort—despite my traditional proclivities—will attempt to explore and channel and reflect that perhaps surprisingly hopeful ardor.

For me, progressive Tar Heel promise is revealed in four principal ways. The first is the most obvious and irrefutable: in election results. Roy Cooper has just completed two four-year terms as a popular and successful Democratic governor. He was accompanied by a twice-elected Democrat in the state's second most important office, attorney general, who was then himself elected governor. In November 2024, despite operating on what was perhaps the country's most politically distorted field of play and facing the headwinds of Trump's race against then–Vice President Kamala Harris, Tar Heels elected Josh Stein (governor), Rachel Hunt (lieutenant governor), Jeff Jackson (attorney general), Elaine Marshall (secretary of state), Mo Green (superintendent of public instruction), and Allison Riggs (supreme court justice). All of them are Democrats, dominating the most important statewide races, where ruthlessly gerrymandered political districts could hold no sway. And though Republicans won two-thirds or nearly two-thirds of the seats in both houses of the General Assembly, more North Carolinians voted for Democrats to represent them in the state legislature than voted for Republicans (which is a remarkable sentence to write, I'll concede). So, blood flows in the North Carolina Democratic Party even if it is forced to flow uphill. And that is really beginning to piss off, and energize, folks from Murphy to Manteo. We pushed back at the darkness in 2024 and managed a meaningful glimpse of the light. I'm confident it will grow. Maybe others aren't, but I am. These victories will produce others—larger ones.

Second, there is the way Republicans choose to run (or, I would suggest, the way they believe they are forced to run) in North Carolina to prevail. I want, of course, to put this gingerly. Reviewing courts have frequently found that the justifications put forward by Republican lawmakers to support their various constraints on constitutional liberties are mere pretext, façade, sham. In other words, they are lies. Apparently, North Carolina Republicans are now convinced they must campaign and govern by perjury, by the lie.

Famously, when, soon after taking unimpeded power in 2013, the General Assembly passed a massive (or, as pundits put it, "monster") voter suppression statute, lawmakers explained to the public, and to federal courts, that the law was simply a common-sense measure designed to eliminate voter fraud and ensure the accuracy of the ballot. But upon examination, federal judges concluded that the bill had nothing whatsoever to do with voter fraud. In fact, former Judge Diana Gribbon Motz wrote, "The state failed to identify even a single individual who had ever been charged with in-person voter fraud in North Carolina." Lawmakers had simply reviewed a wide array of voting processes and restricted those that were used more by Black people and expanded or liberalized those that were utilized more by white people. The handiwork was accomplished with "surgical precision." The goal of the statute wasn't, in the slightest, ballot accuracy; it was to disenfranchise Black people.

That's perhaps a too-long example of my decidedly simpler point: You can't pass a statute and say that your goal is to discriminate against Black people. No matter how much you might believe in that particular endeavor. The public and the courts wouldn't stand for it. So you are, pragmatically, forced to turn to façade, to pretext. And since 2010, pretext has become North Carolina Republicans' principal way of politicking; a central component of Tar Heel Republicanism is lying about what you're after.

Republicans passed a bathroom bill, the notorious House Bill 2, they claimed, not because it was essential to humiliate transgender folks but allegedly to protect women from terrifying assaults in our bathrooms—though no such assaults were ever discovered. They passed the infamous "motorcycle vagina" bill, significantly limiting abortion rights, because its proponents were, for the first time in their lives, incredibly concerned about the health of people who seek abortions. Republicans cut poor kids off food stamps, supposedly to help them out and improve the moral dignity of their parents. North Carolina became the first state to end its earned income tax credit, thus raising the taxes of working families making about $35,000 per year, purportedly to help low-income folks thrive. They eliminated the estate tax under the guise of protecting small farms and businesses, not the big boys.

Republican leaders have worked tirelessly, for fifteen years, to destroy the public school system in North Carolina. But each campaign season, they prepare ads attesting to their unvarnished support for teachers and public schools. After November, they return to their habitual assault. Tar Heels don't support the destruction of public schools; they're committed to public schools. So, the lie has to be deployed. And, most pervasively, North Carolina Republican lawmakers live, foundationally, joyfully, solely, to cut taxes for the richest Tar Heels. It is their only core, absolutist principle. It is the driving force of every legislative session, year in and year out. It always will be. But when it comes to the commanding oligarchic agenda, mums the word. It might be the only thing Republicans truly long for. But you can't go to the people on Election Day with a platform that serves only the top 1 or 2 percent. It's not in the numbers. So, pretext is in order. In fact, it's required.

I've always thought it must be exhausting to govern and campaign by pretext. As Mark Twain put it, "If you tell the truth, you don't have to remember anything." But why do I claim this defining North Carolina Republican characteristic as a basis for optimism? It's complicated, I'll concede. But the deception is born in a sort of compliment to Tar Heel voters even if it is a decidedly backhanded one. Republicans know you can't campaign successfully on hatred and malice in North Carolina. You might be able to in Texas or Alabama, Mississippi or Florida, or closer to home in South Carolina. But it won't work in the real Carolina. You have to make up something else, no matter how absurd the cover is. And that means, even in the Trump era, there's a good future for enthusiastic, aggressive truth-telling in North Carolina. And we're getting better at it.

Third, and related. North Carolina is, in fact, different. North Carolina has long been regarded, or characterized, as "a beacon of southern progress" or a purported "paragon of southern moderation." At least, it used to be. Of course, the moniker of southern moderate has always been bold overstatement, wishful thinking. Any state that was home to the Wilmington coup of 1898, the Greensboro massacre, and North Carolina's brutal record of racial lynchings can't fit comfortably in a sentence with the word "moderate"—and certainly not "beacon of progress."

Still, there is something to the distinguishing sentiment. North

Carolina had Terry Sanford as governor, who endorsed John
Kennedy for president and pushed the North Carolina Fund,
while Alabama boasted George Wallace Jr., who proclaimed "segregation now, segregation tomorrow, and segregation forever."
Maybe more important, North Carolina was home to Frank Porter Graham, Bill Friday, Pauli Murray, Ella Baker, Floyd McKis-
sick Sr. (and junior), Henry Frye, Julius Chambers, Reginald
Hawkins, Jim Hunt, John Hope Franklin, Dean Smith, Rosanell
Eaton, and Maya Angelou.

And there is, as ever, significant blood pumping in the North
Carolina progressive movement. Moral Mondays didn't grow in
the state by accident. Rev. William Barber is a singular leader, the
most remarkable I've been honored to know. But he found fertile
soil in North Carolina, like others had before him. And North
Carolina progressives carry an ever-ready willingness to fight for
their state's future. Even as I wrote this chapter, protestors occu-
pied every corner of the state, fighting to ensure that a soulless
Republican NC Court of Appeals judge wouldn't be allowed to
literally steal a 2024 NC Supreme Court election. Eventually, as
I'll explain, he failed in his venture. But this is North Carolina,
and that means it was entirely possible that he could have been
able to cheat his way onto the high court. If he had, I'm guessing
he would have come to wish he hadn't bothered. Tar Heels aren't
taken with thieves. And they don't suffer such pilfering in silence.

There is also much heroism in the North Carolina Democratic
Party ranks—new and old, high and low. I'm always inspired by
the grit and steel of its best soldiers, and the Democratic legis-

lative caucuses in Raleigh show more heart, nerve, and inspiration than they get credit for (even from me). I'm also much impressed by Anderson Clayton and the other new (mostly young) officers of the state party. I've begun to think that their brand of engaged, community-based politics might eventually merge movement and partisan efforts in the Tar Heel State. That would ensure Democratic majorities large enough to successfully combat even the most artful gerrymanders.

Fourth, and perhaps related, as I'll explain in a couple of different ways, North Carolina Republican leaders seem to have rather dramatically overplayed their hand. Both the General Assembly and the (equally Republican) NC Supreme Court have repeatedly interfered—directly, overtly, illegally, unconstitutionally, I'd even say seditiously (if you believe that trying to destroy democracy in the United States is seditious, as Lincoln did)—with the ability of Tar Heels to elect their own leaders. As is their habit, they lied about their intentions. But so blatant, so astonishing, so outside the traditions of governance were their actions that North Carolinians now understand precisely what they're after. Some support it, no doubt, because they want Republicans to govern; come what may. But new masses of North Carolinians are both enraged (especially) and engaged in every crook and corner of the state. They're eager to fight back in ways not before anticipated. I think Republicans will learn to regret having come out of hiding.

And, to be sure, the stakes in our struggle are beyond high. The defeat of constitutional democracy in North Carolina is

not a mere theoretical or proceduralist wound. As the last fifteen
years have well proven, the suppression of democratic government in the state means that the participatory, adjudicatory, and
dignitary rights of African Americans will be cruelly diminished.
It means that impoverished Tar Heels will be further targeted by
those who are sworn to faithfully represent them. It will result,
again, in evangelical Christians being offered special privileges
that are denied to the rest of the citizenry. Reproductive rights
will be radically degraded or eliminated. Immigrants and members of the LGBTQ+ community will repeatedly be treated as
strangers, outcasts of the commonwealth. Public schools will be
sapped of essential resources by one of the most extreme, and ex-
tremely unaccountable, voucher programs in the United States.
Governing boards of state universities will continue to be rendered hyperpartisan, demolishing academic freedom and free ex-
pression while hypocritically offering paeans to the First Amendment. Local governments will be made to further surrender
traditional authorities before tides of centralized partisan hege-
mony. And threats to safety, health, and the climate will stand
unaddressed as the interests of wealth and consumption bar regulation that is essential to protect our future and that of our children. Defeated democracy means that an empowered minority
of Republican Tar Heels manage to govern in stark violation of
Article I, Section 2 of the North Carolina State Constitution's
recognition that "all political power is derived from the people
and is instituted solely for the good of the whole."

  It is also important to remember that the challenge of distorted or debilitated democracy in North Carolina may well prove to be an enduring one. I'll concede that I am among those who think it possible, or perhaps even likely, that Trump's radical, immensely reckless, destructive, and purposely brutal war against constitutional democracy and traditions of separated powers will implode. After months of Trump's unique and consuming admixture of spite, incompetence, cluelessness, and unbridled greed, it may well become apparent to the nation (or enough of it) that the forty-seventh president is unfit to govern and is wreaking intolerable havoc and hardship on the nation and the world. And, as a result, Trumpist constitutional destruction, one way or another, may well be surprisingly adjudged a massive failure and dissipate or combust.

But, my point is that, even if that were to occur, it is not clear that NC Senate President Pro Tempore Phil Berger and his Republican colleagues will abandon the vise grip they have constructed and presently enjoy over constitutional democracy in the Tar Heel State. Their antidemocratic crusade began five years before Trump descended the golden escalator in 2015. They have also proven to be decidedly more skilled, more patient, more "professional" (if that word can be used), and less obviously vicious and hate driven in their handiwork. Tar Heels are, therefore, decidedly less horrified by it than they are by Trump's unyielding and humiliating cascade of transgressions. I think it likely, therefore, that even if Trump's second presidency involuntarily detonates, North Carolinians will still be faced with the muscular, democracy-defying mechanisms that have been embraced by Republican lawmakers in the state since 2010. We're required to dismantle them on our own. And as we've regularly had proven to us, none of our national cohorts and no court, state or federal, will come to our much-needed rescue.

And here, finally, for once, federalism may be our friend. Southern states have had a barbarous relationship with federalism, or states' rights. We have cuddled up next to it to harbor our most unspeakable sins. It's our habit. But the shield of deception is not the only use of federalism. Ironically, the states present one of our constitutional system's most potent guardrails against the assumption of unlimited federal power. The states are not empty vessels. They can deploy powerful, localized institutions to resist attempted authoritarianism and to model constitutional traditions and mores. They can teach and insist upon standards of democracy and kinship. Present-day struggles over cooperation, or perhaps commandeering, of state officers, provide ready examples.

And beyond such precatory safekeeping, former US Supreme Court Justice Louis Brandeis wrote famously in 1932, "It is one of the happy incidents of our federal system that a single courageous state may, if its citizens choose, serve as a laboratory, and try novel social and economic experiments without risk to the rest of the country." He might have added "without risk or permission *from* the rest of the nation."

That means, one hopes, that regardless of what transpires in Washington, DC, North Carolina is free to build, in Frank Porter Graham's words, "a nobler and fresher civilization in this ancient commonwealth." We are not *required* to target the most vulnerable among us or to cling to the worst indignities of our past. Not every state in the union totters on the edge of lost democracy. Many states happily face the challenges of new centuries without longing to resurrect the transgressions and hypocrisies of decades and centuries gone. Republican leaders of the last decade and a half have sought, overtly, to ensure that the Tar Heel State is "economically competitive" in our own region. But, of course, the South is the native home of poverty in the United States. That means we have always had more low-income people and more political leaders who are utterly untroubled by that demoralizing fact than the rest of the country. It is not demanded that it be so. We are not required to marry ourselves to the same version of feudalism that our neighbors claim to enjoy.

North Carolina can set its own course. We can govern ourselves. We don't have to settle for the lowest southern denominator. We can choose to be better, live better, strive better. We can provide a better life for our children, for our sisters and brothers. We can choose to escape the shadows. We have much to seek. And getting there is not barred to us. It is time to contribute our chapter to a civilization that is "nobler" and "fresher." And if that is to be our goal, then the path forward lies clearly in our own hands and on our own backs. As Ella Baker, another teaching and sacrificing Tar Heel, instructed us, the most crucial work is not done "until we can get people to recognize that they themselves have to make the struggle and they have to make the fight for freedom every day in the year, every year, until they win it." Then, perhaps, we can urge our neighbors to come along.

This short book, then, attempts to help identify an agenda for North Carolina progressives to combat their state's Republican destruction. Its chapters offer proposals that are aimed at recovering and reasserting our democratic traditions and commitments to limited government and separated, structurally checked, powers. They call, as well, for a foundational demand to ensure the full dignity and equal membership of all Tar Heels. They also link claims of economic justice; rights to support, sustain, and educate our children; and the shared goal of securing a healthy, safe, and sustainable natural world for ourselves and our successors.

Chapter 2 necessarily sets forth the emboldened attack on constitutional democracy that is presently and successfully underway at the hands of North Carolina's Republican General Assembly and the hideously partisan, utterly nonjudicial, NC Supreme Court. These aren't my favorite topics. But it is vital to look our challenges, and our now-committed antidemocratic adversaries, directly in the eye. It does us no service to pretend that our defining commitment as a people is not decidedly threatened and already patently wounded.

But the main impetus of these pages is to explore what idealistic and steely committed North Carolinians ought to do about it. And the remainder of the chapters explore some of those possibilities.

Chapter 3 outlines claims for a defined and implemented right to equal political participation for all North Carolinians, directly challenging the abusive electoral transgressions experienced in the state over the last decade and a half. Chapter 4 explores essential challenges to ensure an independent and accountable judicial system in a state that has, at present, lost its own. Chapter 5 turns to critical and foundational guarantees of full membership and dignity for all Tar Heels, particularly focusing on now-contested rights to reproductive freedom and intimate, personal privacy. Even if the US Supreme Court has turned its back on these most vital liberties, North Carolinians, I'm convinced, will not.

Chapter 6 focuses on economic matters, seeking to push back against North Carolina's now potently established proclivity for governing only in the interest of the wealthy—governing, usually covertly, for the richest among us. Even southerners, I'll claim, are warm to economic justice. And we're certainly not taken with being played for fools.

Chapter 7 explores one of North Carolina's, or any state's, most crucial challenges: how we support, secure, and educate our children. Here, once again, our record embarrasses us. And it embarrasses us for similar reasons: refusing to give full credence, full opportunity, and full membership to the most disadvantaged among us and turning away from the most foundational notion of our history and traditions, which is the belief in the sanctity of all God's children. In the final substantive chapter, I try to modestly extend these lessons to the sustainability of our natural world, both today and tomorrow.

Chapter 9, the conclusion, speaks to what most matters and

will most make the necessary difference: the obligation of North Carolina's engaged citizenry to fight for its future—the charge that this generation of Tar Heels, like generations before it, will rise to assert its dignity, its courage, its character, its commitment to its children, and its defining fealty to the democratic experiment to defeat the Republican crusade to end free government in North Carolina. And make no mistake; free government is what is on the line—today.

I attempt, in each instance, to offer proposals and recommendations that are straightforward, comprehensible, and capable of being pursued through the operations of the political process. In most chapters, I include proffered state constitutional amendments that might serve to focus debate and electoral attention on the needed reforms as well as secure democratic values into the future. I try to join a call to arms with at least some specifics of what I think of as a progressive Tar Heel agenda. My hope, of course, is to add a few notions to our foundational and now notably endangered exercises in self-government. As we say in Chapel Hill, "Hark the Sound."

## CHAPTER TWO

★ ★ ★

# Crushing Constitutional Democracy
# in North Carolina

E ven at the risk of violating my disclaimer, I should be clear that I make no claim that any threat to democracy in the United States comes close to that posed by President Donald Trump—not anywhere in the country, not at any time since the Civil War. It would be a life's work to even attempt to rank his astonishing transgressions. He tried to instigate a violent coup against the lawful government of the nation. He issued pardons to 1,500 assailants who followed his brutal call, showing his embrace of murderous, seditious insurrection so long as it is carried out on his behalf. He then exacted a purge of the Department of Justice officers who successfully prosecuted his fellow coup participants. He said that the members of the January 6 congressional committee who investigated the outrages should be imprisoned. He demanded, on tape, like a mafioso, that Georgia's secretary of state steal 11,000 votes to fraudulently overturn the 2020 election. He required that an entire national political party avow, in obvious and undeniable falsity, that the 2020 presidential election was stolen. And worse, the Republican Party agreed, in humiliating and disqualifying submission.

On the first day of his second term, Trump issued an executive order attempting to override the Fourteenth Amendment. Soon thereafter, he unleashed the richest man in the world, without authority, legality, or accountability, to single-handedly dismantle the US government, sacrificing the lives and well-beings of the poorest people on the face of the earth. He threatened to invade Greenland, Panama, and Canada, like a mad, imperialist, eighteenth-century monarch. He demanded that the United States embrace the ancient description from Thucydides: "The strong do what they can, and the weak suffer what they must." Literally nothing could be more un-American. His administration has violated the Constitution with impunity and refused to follow orders of the United States Supreme Court. He has instituted a police state wherein residents are seized on the streets and in their homes, places of work, schools, and churches without a shred of process and then are summarily shipped to foreign lands never to be heard from again. He has deployed the military in US cities as if it were his personal strike force. He has openly embraced a regime of corruption that has never before been approached in the United States. And he governs through a reign of terror and extortion that demands control of every segment of US life—the press, universities, law firms, corporations, nonprofits—nothing, he believes, should be deemed beyond his grasp. Not to mention his thirty-four felonies and sexual assault.

No one has a record to match this. Aaron Burr, Jefferson Davis, and Nathan Bedford Forrest were many things. But none were president of the United States.

## The North Carolina Way

But our focus here is North Carolina and its more mannerly anti-democratic crusade. The bare bones of this story are, in one sense, familiar to many. In 2008, North Carolina voted for a Barack Obama presidency. A potent political backlash ensued. In 2010, Republicans, by wide margins, took over both houses of the General Assembly. Two years later, they captured the governor's office as well. For the first time since 1870, Republicans controlled all three branches of government in the Tar Heel State. Change rolled in.

Broadly speaking, the altered course was seen as politically conservative, even radically so: attacking public schools, trying to eliminate teacher tenure, restricting abortion rights, expanding gun rights, dramatically cutting social programs, slashing legal aid, passing internationally derided limitations on the LGBTQ+ community, refusing to expand Medicaid under the Patient Protection and Affordable Care Act for a decade, enacting the largest cut to a state unemployment compensation scheme in history, placing searing restrictions on food assistance, requiring drug tests for benefits applicants, eliminating the state's earned income tax credit, and increasing regressive sales taxes all while repeatedly doling out massive tax cuts to the wealthiest North Carolinians and out-of-state corporations. In short, moving from what national pundits had long deemed a progressive beachhead in the South to "a poster child for regressive, conservative policies." The *New York Times* noted our "pioneering work in bigotry." The *Washington Post* concluded that our General Assembly "had turned back 50 years of progress on civil rights and gutted the social safety net."

If civil rights and social welfare programs sustained famous and internationally noted body blows, the newly Republican General Assembly's war on democratic processes was equally enthusiastic and perhaps even more relentless. Upon assuming power in 2011, its essentially all-white Republican caucuses moved quickly to distort the electoral playing field by targeting African Americans. Federal reviewing courts concluded that the lawmakers' redistricting statutes represented "widespread, serious and longstanding constitutional violations [that were] among the largest racial gerrymanders ever encountered by a federal court." And because the General Assembly fought relentlessly, over years, to retain its racially biased electoral schemes, the judges determined that "the persistent and malignant effects extended well beyond the voting booth."

Voters were repeatedly separated into "geographical boundaries [which] bore an uncomfortable resemblance to political apartheid." Because the denials of equality were "inflicted again and again, in each subsequent election cycle, legislators were put into office under a cloud of constitutional illegitimacy." Another court noted that "as James Madison warned, a legislature that is itself insulated by virtue of its invidious gerrymanders can enact additional legislation to restrict voting rights and thereby firmly cement its unjustified control of the organs of both federal and state government."

Almost on cue, in 2016, the Republican General Assembly passed a massive voter suppression bill that was characterized by election law scholars as the most restrictive enacted by any state or federal legislature in a half-century. It ended same-day registration, shortened early voting periods, eliminated student registration programs, and, more notably, included a racially slanted voter identification requirement. Judges concluded that the principal motivation for the legislative restrictions was to burden Black people. And it did that work energetically: "Neither this legislature nor, as far as we can tell, any other has ever done so much, so fast, to restrict access to the franchise," judges determined.

The racialized Republican caucuses of the General Assembly also soon repealed the landmark North Carolina Racial Justice Act of 2009; moved to prohibit the teaching of critical race theory; ended university diversity, equity, and inclusion (DEI) programs; enacted special punishments for Black Lives Matter protestors; made it harder to obtain access to police-camera footage; made Confederate memorials sacrosanct; and generously subsidized discriminatory private K–12 schools. The North Carolina Republicans' ambitious pattern of race-based discrimination in electoral districting continues unabated. A new federal lawsuit will be tried in 2025.

Given North Carolina's often brutal history of racial oppression, and its continuing landscape of massive racial disparities, it is perhaps stunning that one of its primary governing political parties would adopt the suppression of African Americans as a central component of its statewide policy agenda. It is now unsurprising, though, that reviewing federal courts conclude that the Republican General Assembly's record of racial performance "raises legitimate questions regarding the [lawmakers'] capacity or willingness" to achieve constitutional compliance. The lawmakers' statutory record has also compromised "popular sovereignty," effectively eroding the essential requirements of government by consent of the governed. The principal author of the Fourteenth Amendment, post–Civil War Republican Rep. John Bingham, called it "a simple, strong, plain declaration that equal laws and exact justice shall be secured within every state for any person, no matter whence he comes, or how poor, how weak, how simple, how friendless." After the Civil War, North Carolina initially refused to ratify the Fourteenth Amendment. Our Republicans leaders are now out to do it in again, a century and a half later.

Having determined that its efforts in racial voter suppression were too frequently hindered, or at least delayed, by the federal courts, in 2016, the General Assembly also turned to a bold regime of politically partisan gerrymandering, creatively drawing election district lines to favor Republican candidates. The country's leading election law expert, Richard Hasen, deemed it "the most brazen and egregious [set of] political gerrymanders yet seen in the United States." The legislative author of the redistricting plans explained, "I think electing Republicans is better than electing Democrats, so I drew the maps to foster what I think is better for the country." He offered a congressional map that was designed, in an evenly divided state, to deliver ten Republican congressional seats and three Democratic seats. He did so only as a concession to the limitations of human capacity, not "believing it possible to draw a map with 11 Republicans and two Democrats." Commentators like Michael Li were modestly stunned by such unembarrassed braggadocio. He wrote that "North Carolina Republicans didn't just get caught red-handed robbing the bank, they had a press conference beforehand and said, 'We are going to rob the bank.'"

Such extreme partisan gerrymanders were initially held to violate the state constitution by the North Carolina Supreme Court. But in 2023, the state high tribunal changed to Republican hands. And the new majority quickly gave a complete and vivid green light to political gerrymandering, no matter how radical or distorting. Republican Chief Justice Paul Newby, surely the most partisan chief justice in North Carolina history, determined that our state constitution is unbothered by lawmakers permanently entrenching themselves in power regardless of the wishes of the voters. Fixing elections to predetermine the winners is no transgression—if the politicians who are entrenched are Republicans. The North Carolina State Constitution guarantees that "all elections shall be free." But, for Newby, a merely rigged election is still a "free election." So, if lawmakers cheat in drawing election lines because they "think electing Republicans is better than electing Democrats," then it's no problem. Literally, it is no problem. Stacking the deck in North Carolina, as of 2023, is perfectly legal. According to the Republican justices of our state's high court, it is apparently even admirable. Boys will be boys, and politicians will debilitate democracy. Though I'm guessing the Get Out of Jail Free card only runs in one political direction.

North Carolinians have seen such distortion in operation. After the NC Supreme Court offered free reign to the General Assembly to cheat in the drawing of district lines, in a 50–50 state, the Tar Heel congressional delegation switched from an even 7–7 split to a 10–4 Republican advantage in the 2024 elections. The slanted maps thus helped deliver a Republican majority in the United States House of Representatives in 2025. Though Democratic candidates prevailed in almost all the major statewide races, Republicans, with the benefit of extreme partisan gerrymandered districts, won huge majorities in both chambers of the General Assembly. All told, most voters cast their ballots for Democrats, but still, Republicans obtained a powerfully distorted edge in membership. Democrats got the votes; Republicans got the seats. Cheating works. So grotesque is North Carolina Republican gerrymandering that Democratic lawmakers, both state and federal, cannot achieve majority representation with even a significant majority of the state's votes. This surely pleases NC Senate President Phil Berger and perhaps his son, Philip Berger Jr., a justice of the North Carolina Supreme Court, but it is not democracy. As the *New York Times* has written, North Carolina "has become a paradigm of unrepresentative democracy." Rachel Maddow calls the Tar Heel State the Republicans' "anti-democratic pilot project."

## Obliterating the Guardrails:
## Ending the Separation of Powers

North Carolina Republicans haven't been satisfied with systematically and pervasively rigging elections. Pathbreaking discrimination against Black citizens and Democrats hasn't been good enough. The greediest transgressor always seems to demand more. That greed, that power lust, has also led the Republican North Carolina General Assembly to dismantle the state's constitutionally mandated separation of powers. Article I, Section 6 of the North Carolina State Constitution declares confidently, "The legislative, executive and supreme judicial powers of the State government shall be forever separate and distinct from each other." North Carolina Republicans have read that clear, foundational mandate to mean that "all powers reside in the General Assembly"—so long as they control it. Through a series of "sore loser laws" and bald usurpations of protected executive authorities, North Carolina's traditional and constitutionally announced government structure has been left for dust. As a result, North Carolina's elections, already tainted, have often been rendered farcical charades. And the foundational liberties of Tar Heels— particularly the most basic of all democratic norms, the right to be free from tyrannical, all-consuming government power—have been stunningly threatened in the process.

It is perhaps too obvious to state, but you can't rig a statewide election by cheating in the drawing of districts. There is but one district: the state in its entirety. You might make it harder for your adversaries to vote, or limit access to polling places, or alter early voting availability, or try to control the election commission, or the like. North Carolina Republicans have done all these and more. Still, their performance in statewide races has disappointed them. When this has occurred, Republican lawmakers have repeatedly turned to what other states have deemed "the North Carolina plan." I think of it as a now-familiar North Carolina two-step.

If the people of North Carolina had the temerity to elect a Democratic governor, Phil Berger and former Speaker of the NC House of Representatives Tim Moore and their crews immediately began the process of stripping the chief executive of essential powers. *We'll show 'em*, the theory goes. There's no need to turn over the keys to the governor's mansion; just burn the place down.

When Democrat Roy Cooper III was elected for the first time in 2016, Republican lawmakers searched, but couldn't find, a way to overturn the result. Instead, they triggered an immediate special session and began gutting Cooper's powers. They reduced the number of positions in the governor's office from 1,000 to 425. They required, for the first time, that cabinet department secretaries be confirmed by the state senate. The governor's power to appoint university trustees was eliminated. Both state and local election boards were reconstituted, diminishing gubernatorial authority and delivering it to Republicans. The NC State Ethics Commission was altered. Later, lawmakers removed the governor's power to appoint the majority of such significant executive commissions as the Environmental Management Commission, the Coastal Resources Commission, and the Building Code Council. State policy expert Ran Coble called it "death by a thousand cuts" to constitutionally ensured executive powers. National commentators were less gracious, deeming it "a legislative coup," "the kind of thing one might expect to see in Venezuela, not in a U.S. state, an attack on democracy itself."

When Josh Stein was elected governor by fifteen points in 2024, he received even harsher treatment. Republican lawmakers hijacked a hurricane relief bill, presented in a special session immediately before they lost their supermajority in the General Assembly, to radically restructure the state government and deplete the powers of the governor and the other Council of State Democrats who had just been elected. If North Carolina voters had demanded a divided government, Republican lawmakers showed that they wouldn't hear of it. Phil Berger and Tim Moore would decide who governs North Carolina, by hook or by crook—mostly by crook, as it turns out.

In December 2024, Senate Bill 382 stripped from offices, that were to be held by Democrats in less than a month, an array of essential, long-held executive powers and redirected much of the authority to Republicans. The most noted and controversial provision relieved incoming Governor Stein of the power to appoint and oversee the NC State Board of Elections.

The board of elections had been something of a holy grail for
Senator Berger. He had a go at it six times in eight years. He attempted to remove the election commission appointment authority previously, but his effort was blocked, unsurprisingly,
by the state courts. Republicans proposed a similar takeover
through a proffered constitutional amendment in 2016, but the
voters rejected it by more than 60 percent. With Senate Bill
382, State Senator Berger, after having made a mockery of North
Carolina elections through the infliction of extreme partisan
gerrymandering, claimed that he just wanted to take over the
board of elections to make it "fair."

This time, the Republicans, almost comically, gave the governor's appointment power to the state auditor. That wise policy
choice only became obvious when Republican David Boliek Jr.
won the auditor's race a few weeks before. With SB 382, North
Carolina became the first (and only) state to lodge election over-
sight in the state auditor's office. I wonder why? Next year, perhaps, the commissioner of agriculture, a Republican, will become
"the commander-in-chief of the state military" and the commissioner of insurance, another member of the Grand Old Party,
will get the pardon power.

The election commission remake was as unconstitutional as
the day is long. The NC State Constitution declares "the executive power of the state shall be vested in the Governor" (Article
III, Section 1). The governor, and no one else, has the "power to
take care that the law be faithfully executed" (Article III, Section
5). Tar Heels have one governor. They don't expect the auditor

to do the governor's job. No one actually believes that they do. SB 382 demonstrates, literally, that there are no limits to what North Carolina Republicans will do in pursuit of boundless power—even if their claimed justification is absurd.

SB 382 also limited the power of the governor to appoint various judges and restricted his authority to oversee the North Carolina State Highway Patrol. It took various powers over the NC Utilities Commission and State Board of Education away from the governor as well, transferring them to other newly elected Republicans. As was the case with the auditor designation, the newly empowered Republicans' offices need not have had anything whatsoever to do with the tasks of the refashioned agency. All that mattered was that the governor's responsibilities were shifted to Republican adversaries. No doubt, the deck will be reshuffled after the next election as well to match any pesky changes in electoral outcomes. If only one member of the Council of State elected in 2028 is a Republican, they should be prepared to take over the entirety of the governor's authority. It would only be "fair." It's not necessary that North Carolina voters have any conceivable idea what responsibilities the next person they choose as governor will actually be allowed to retain, if any. That's to be decided by Phil Berger—after the electoral count comes in. Constitutional government in North Carolina exists, if it does at all, only under the generous grace of the Republican General Assembly. Former President James Madison wrote, in *The Federalist Papers* (no. 47), "The accumulation of all powers, legislative, executive, and judiciary, in the same hands may justly be pronounced the very definition of tyranny." North Carolina Republicans must think Madison was a chump—or a prophet.

Almost as if to emphasize the point, when Trump issued, in the first weeks of his second term, a series of executive orders that were meant to demolish the tradition of separation of powers, Republican lawmakers in North Carolina introduced a bill declaring, "The Attorney General shall not advance any argument in an action pending before a state or federal court that would result in the invalidation of any statute enacted by the General Assembly or any executive order issued by the President of the United States."

Power-stripping arrangements like those in SB 382, of course, also give the back of the hand to North Carolina voters. They violate, outrageously, both the equal protection clause of the Fourteenth Amendment and Article IV, Section 4's requirement that "the United States shall guarantee to every State in the Union a Republican Form of Government." That's true whether folks like Berger, Moore, their state supreme court buddies, and the whole Republican Party agree or not. Our country's founders believed in those guarantees strongly enough to put them in the US Constitution. Most of us still believe in them.

## A Supreme Court's Complicity

The abuses of extreme and racialized gerrymandering, compounded by astonishingly ambitious legislative power grabs that rob executive offices of their core functions, might not prove fatal to a state's system of democratic government if their impacts were limited, or even thwarted, by an actual independent state supreme court. Since 2023, North Carolina hasn't had one.

In the November 2022 election, Republican candidates flipped a 4–3 Democratic majority to 5–2 Republican. Trey Allen defeated incumbent Justice Sam Ervin IV, and Richard Dietz outpolled Democratic Court of Appeals Judge Lucy Inman. Philip Berger Jr., already an incumbent member of the high tribunal and the senate majority leader's son, celebrated the "lasting grip of the Republican Party on the North Carolina Supreme Court" in a footnote of a dissenting opinion. I've been reading appellate opinions for almost fifty years. I've never seen anything like that.

Almost immediately upon the seating of its new members, the now-Republican North Carolina Supreme Court began issuing unprecedented "re-hearing" orders to reverse an array of final rulings of its predecessor. The high court had never used the re-hearing process in such a manner in its more than 200-year history. Then, following the stunning ditching of its rules of appellate review, the Republican justices announced a much-ballyhooed troika of political decisions in an April 2023 coming-out party. *Harper v. Hall*, *Holmes v. Moore*, and *Community Success Initiative v. Moore* overturned prior rulings invalidating extreme partisan gerrymandering, racially motivated voter identification requirements, and various protections against felony disenfranchisement. The decisions were launched as a group purportedly reflecting what the justices described as a necessary "course correction," returning the state judiciary to "its designated lane." No longer would the

Court "thrust itself" into political disputes. The judicial role was to be "realigned." In one of the opinions, Justice Phillip Berger Jr., who, amazingly, refuses to recuse himself from cases in which his daddy is a party, declared haughtily that, from now on, "Our state courts will follow the law, not the political winds of the day." It read like a story from *The Onion*. No greater falsehood could have been spoken.

In the series of rulings, the Republican justices explained that the North Carolina General Assembly, home of their political benefactors, was, in fact, the "great and chief department of government" in the Tar Heel State. Justices, therefore, owed massive "deference to acts of the General Assembly as their legislative enactments represent the sacrosanct fulfillment of the people's will." *Sacrosanct*. Accordingly, generous presumptions of constitutional compliance and legislative good faith must be deployed by all reviewing judges—despite a federal court's earlier declaration that the track record of the North Carolina General Assembly demonstrated a "lack of willingness and capacity" to comply with the Constitution of the United States. North Carolina justices showed the "utmost restraint" in constitutional decision-making to defend against any conceivable "abuse of judicial power." A new sheriff was in town. No longer would state courts intervene to protect voting rights. No longer would they fret over the intentional distortion of the political process. No longer, even more broadly, would the justices trouble the Republican General Assembly to govern between constitutional lines.

No longer would they offer even the pretense of independent judicial review. It was understood that the North Carolina Supreme Court would behave only as an obedient caucus of the Republican Party. And since their ascendancy in 2023, on this front at least, the Republican majority has been true to its obsequious pledge.

## Defeating Democracy through a Vise Grip of Transgression

The marriage of a Republican General Assembly that regularly uses its disproportionate and illegitimately garnered legislative authority to crush the guardrails of constitutional government with a hyperpartisan state supreme court that refuses to enforce explicitly mandated, foundational standards of separation of powers draws ever more power to the state legislature, dismantles the traditional structures of North Carolina government, and works to diminish or overturn election results that lawmakers deplore. It also allows Republicans to effectively debilitate the one branch of government (the executive branch) that they don't already control.

Broadly speaking, and unfortunately, state separation-of-powers issues are typically left in the hands of state supreme courts in legal decision-making and are unreviewable by the federal judiciary. So when our state supreme court determines that the General Assembly can do whatever it wants, including cheat by redistricting and override the results of elections through sore loser laws regardless of the clear limitations of the North Carolina State Constitution, the people of the Tar Heel State are left without effective legal or political recourse. Such are the wages of state judges who intentionally refuse to do their jobs and state lawmakers whose efforts are driven only by the ambitions of power and tribe. The perilous combination creates, in North Carolina today, a type of vicious circle, a feedback loop, a reinforcing cascade of transgression that moves beyond partisan gamesmanship toward the destruction of our central, defining heritage—what Lincoln and Jefferson thought of as the defining urge of human beings, self-government itself. This is the unfolding, or now-unfolded, plan of the Republican leadership of the North Carolina General Assembly. It is not carried out through threats of violence or taunts of hatred and menace, like the antidemocratic crusades of Trump and his expanding troop of seditionists in Washington, DC. But North Carolina's version of constitutional suppression is every bit as ambitious and, potentially, effective as its more overtly venomous, and more obvious, counterpart. It does Tar Heels no service to pretend otherwise.

North Carolina Republicans now believe, with this combination of legislative and judicial abuse, that they can defeat constitutional democracy in the Tar Heel State. In this, as in so much else, they are wrong, deadly wrong. But their ambitions are more than mistaken. They also shame themselves and demonstrate their unfitness to govern. They seek to crush the meaning and mission of their homeland. In pressing their crusade, they become, in fact, a massive sedition caucus. In that effort, they must be overcome.

I now turn, for the rest of these discussions, to what we might do to defeat them.

## CHAPTER THREE

★ ★ ★

# Siding with the Declaration

## A Right to Equal Political Participation

irst, a reminder: Thomas Jefferson made the Declaration of Independence an aspirational as well as a separational document. He wrote, of course, that "all men are created equal" and are "endowed by their Creator with certain inalienable rights; that among these are life, liberty and the pursuit of happiness." Robert Frost noted, nearly two centuries later, "The Welshman got it planted where it will trouble us for a thousand years ... each generation will have to reconsider it."

Abraham Lincoln saw his presidency, and the Civil War itself, as designed to secure a government "conceived in liberty and dedicated to the proposition" of equality. He sought, overtly, to "readopt the Declaration of Independence and the practices which harmonize with it." For him, these were "the definitions and axioms of a free society." Under the declaration's mandate, the union could "be so saved as to make it worthy of the saving."

Lincoln, of course, knew the declaration's hypocrisies. Its drafters "did not mean to state the obvious untruth that all were actually enjoying that equality, nor yet that they were about to confer it immediately upon them ... they meant simply to declare the right so that enforcement might follow as circumstances permit." They meant to set the "standard for a free society, familiar to all, revered by all, labored for, and even though never perfectly attained, constantly spreading and deepening its influence."

The Civil War, Lincoln explained to Congress, was a "struggle to maintain in the world that form of government whose leading object is to elevate the condition of men, to lift artificial weights from all shoulders, to clear the paths for all. This is the object of the government for whose existence we contend." They fought, he argued, for something "back of the Constitution, entwining itself more closely about the human heart, the principle of 'Liberty to all.'"

Former President Lyndon Johnson put it similarly when introducing the Voting Rights Act of 1965, "This was the first nation in the history of the world to be founded with a purpose. The great phrases of that purpose still sound in every American heart: 'All men are created equal,' 'Government by Consent of the Governed,' 'Give me liberty or give me death.'"

"All are created equal." This is our defining creed, our national mission.

Vice President J. D. Vance, perhaps unsurprisingly, tried to at least divert us from this defining truth in his 2024 Republican National Convention speech: "America is not just an idea. It is a group of people with a shared history and a common future. It is a nation."

That was Vance's ruse for anti-immigrant policies. He thought Lincoln got it wrong, Lincoln and everyone else. We won't be building any memorials to J. D. Vance.

Of course, Lincoln's longed-for march toward "liberty for all" has hardly been linear or nonbrutal; it has proven to be bloody, tragic, and unspeakably grudging. Nor is its success, even ultimately, assured. At every stage, progress has met full-throated and often even malevolent resistance.

North Carolina's history vividly reflects this antiegalitarian pattern. My colleagues Jim Leloudis and Bob Korstad have documented it powerfully. They have demonstrated that since the Civil War, African Americans in the state have repeatedly formed political movements and alliances to combat racial discrimination and achieve overarching rights of equal citizenship. They have additionally sought to enlarge participatory democracy and to press the government to be responsive to the needs of all. "Invariably," the historians wrote, "conservative lawmakers have countered such efforts by erecting barriers around the ballot box." Sometimes calling themselves Democrats, sometimes Republicans, dominant white political forces in North Carolina, often deploying force, have campaigned against measures to address inequality and conspired to defeat broadened rights of suffrage. Reconstruction scholar Eric Foner explained that the "politics of today is continuous with the past that made it, marked by struggles that have never really ended, only shifted and returned." Speak-

ing more broadly, Heather Cox Richardson wrote that throughout our history, the United States "has swung between the defense of equality outlined in the Declaration of Independence
and our peculiar history of racism and property." Every time it
seems "we are approaching equality before law, those determined
to prevent it rise." The electoral handiwork of today's Republican
North Carolina General Assembly fits snuggly into the state's op-
pressive historical template.

North Carolina Republicans' crusade to defeat democracy is
rooted in the rejection of pluralist democracy; the repudiation
of the Declaration of Independence's sweeping promise that "all
are created equal." It is meant to strike against a "rising tide of
demographic change," a tide that threatens Republican strong-
holds among rural, older, non-college-educated, white voters. As
experts have put it, Republicans seek to build a wall against urban population explosions and keep it from "smashing the last
bastion of their dominance." They mean, at all costs, to avoid the
perils of one person, one vote. So, they make it notably harder for
their adversaries to exercise the franchise. They become afficiona-
dos of districting fraud. They tamper with the polling processes
and the election commission. They interfere with judicial elections. They drain executive offices of authority when their adversaries win. Put together, these moves are not that different from a
statute that says that vote counters are required to throw out one
of every three Democratic ballots. If forced to choose between
actual majority rule and their own vested ascendancy, the last de-

cade and a half has proven that Republicans will cast aside democracy in favor of their own permanent power every time.

But nowhere is the crushing Republican grip on authority implemented more directly, more effectively, in North Carolina than in the destructive use of extreme partisan gerrymandering — in deciding who gets the seats regardless of who gets the votes. No one has described the corrosive impact of North Carolina Republican gerrymandering abuse more comprehensively than Justice Elena Kagan of the United States Supreme Court, and former dean of Harvard Law School, in words that were not challenged by her colleagues in *Rucho v. Common Cause*:

> North Carolina partisan gerrymanders have deprived citizens of the most fundamental of their constitutional rights: the rights to participate equally in the political process, to join with others to advance their political beliefs, and to choose their political representatives. In doing so, the partisan gerrymanders debased and dishonored our democracy, turning upside-down the core American idea that all government power derives from the people... enabling politicians to entrench themselves in office as against voters' preferences. They have promoted partisanship above respect for popular will. If left unchecked, [they] may irreparably damage our system of government.

Kagan's 2019 prediction turned out to be quite literally true. As she put it, partisan gerrymandering like North Carolina's can make elections "meaningless." In fact, the actual architect of North Carolina's world-beating gerrymanders, the late Republican gerrymandering expert Thomas Hofeller, laid the process out bare, in writing, years before: "The gerrymander overcometh all. What demographics give, legislatures can take away in the dead of night. [Their maps] were the only legalized form of vote-stealing left in the United States."

And the threat that gerrymandering poses gets worse each passing year. Technological advances have enabled mapmakers to use voter information "with unprecedented efficiency." Each succeeding decade makes the potential for cheating more pronounced. As data becomes "ever more fine-grained and analytical techniques continue to improve," Kagan noted, the threat to equal political participation overwhelms. No fair judge, or fair lawmaker, could believe it tolerable. North Carolina Supreme Court Chief Justice Paul Newby's claim that the meaning of a "free election" in 2025 ought to be measured by some centuries-old interaction with King John in merry old England is so profoundly ludicrous that, if it weren't so "learned," it would be laughed at out loud, deservedly, in a middle-school classroom.

And there's more. In theory, at least, racial gerrymandering is illegal in North Carolina while political gerrymandering, even extreme political gerrymandering, is embraced. But, in truth, it's impossible to separate racial line drawing from partisan districting in the Tar Heel State. When the Republican caucuses of the North Carolina General Assembly retire to their closed-door meetings to draft the laws of the state, and then those highly racialized sessions produce a dramatically racialized statutory regime, year after year, is it really believable to claim that their districting strategies are merely "political" and not racial? Does anyone believe that? No honest person in North Carolina does. So here, at least, it has become essential to eliminate political gerrymandering in order to eliminate racial gerrymandering. They are twins—identical ones.

## Necessity

It is hard, or perhaps even impossible, to overstate the importance of Democrats defeating the curse of partisan gerrymandering in North Carolina—now. It is more than central, really. It is essential, necessary, needed above all else. At present, we play on a fully rigged field. And the field's slant wounds the prospects and possibilities of Tar Heels, particularly the most marginalized ones. I know that many people, especially after the 2024 presidential election, think that restoring democracy is less appealing as a political issue than, say, inflation (or, as it's put, "the price of eggs"). And I argue (in chapter 6) that a consuming attention to pocketbook issues and questions of economic fairness for average North Carolinians, for low- and middle-income folks, must constitute the beating heart of any progressive Democratic agenda. I think, flatly, that Democrats ought to always have a preference for those in the middle and at the bottom of the economic pecking order. And we should leave no voter in doubt on that front.

But without escaping the clutches, the traumas, of a fixed electoral system, nothing else will much matter. And besides, as heirs to this great political experiment, it is our job to restore democracy in North Carolina, just like it was for earlier generations on the beaches of Normandy or on the streets of Selma in their much harder and more perilous tasks. So, the truth is, we are required to overcome the stranglehold on free government regardless of whether everybody else thinks that it is important or not. If some choose not to pay attention, or even are happy to see democracy's demise, that doesn't diminish the duty that the rest of us inherit. It might make it tougher to prevail, but it doesn't alter the task or the calling. We are required to win back our democracy whether everybody else thinks it's crucial or not.

That means that our policy strategy must be made clear and repeated daily. Democrats have to demand, and deliver, at least two profound electoral changes. First, we are obliged to pass a statute prohibiting partisan gerrymandering. I'd put it like this: "North Carolina citizens enjoying the inherent right to free and fair elections, it shall be forever illegal to draw electoral districts that are designed to favor any incumbent or any political party."

I think we ought to write it into the state constitution as well so that we can ensure it for the future against any additional, upcoming seditionists. But we can begin with a statute, one that would be explicit and mandatory and that could not possibly be misunderstood, ignored, or deemed unconstitutional even by the likes of Paul Newby. Though I'm not saying he wouldn't try. But it would be hard for him to invent a rule saying that the people of North Carolina are *required* to help Republicans defeat self-government. The United States Supreme Court, in the North Carolina–born *Rucho* case, implicitly welcomed such no partisanship laws by state legislatures. Nothing could say them nay. And if the radically partisan North Carolina Supreme Court tried to intervene, it would be tough to pull off. It would be hard for them to create a rule announcing that the state constitution allows only one political party in the Tar Heel State, and it must be spelled R-E-P-U-B-L-I-C-A-N. I'm not saying they wouldn't try to do it. I just doubt that they could carry the day.

But, as most folks know, a statute or even a constitutional amendment alone won't do the trick in North Carolina. The massive conflict of interest that is inherent in lawmakers setting the boundaries of their own election districts has been demonstrated here so many times, for so long, so aggressively, by both political parties, even to the destruction of a functioning democracy, that it simply must be ended outright. The people of North Carolina are required to take the power to cheat out of the hands of their lawmakers. Full stop. It is essential to amend the North Carolina State Constitution to require that legislative and congressional districts be drawn by an independent redistricting commission.

An amendment is required because, at present, the state constitution allocates districting authority to the General Assembly. So, a statute creating an independent line-drawing institution alone likely wouldn't do the job. And, unfortunately, North Carolina citizens, unlike the citizens of many other states, do not enjoy the power to alter their state constitution by initiative, which is launched by the people. A measure for an independent redistricting commission would have to be placed on the ballot by referendum, which is controlled by the legislature. And as long as North Carolina Republicans continue to carry the commitment to rig elections as the central tenet of their political agenda, adopting an independent redistricting commission will require that Democrats gain control of the General Assembly. To control it, and to secure the necessary three-fifths-majority vote to place an amendment on the ballot is no easy lift.

The Democratic Legislative Campaign Committee has announced North Carolina as one of its top targets for the 2025–2026 state election cycle. The Democratic National Committee itself has also stepped up its levels of support for the much-contested Tar Heel State. Maybe more telling, Anderson Clayton, North Carolina's inspiring state party chair, has reported that, "Democrats can gain five more state house seats in 2026, primarily in areas where Kamala Harris won the state but Democrats didn't." And, as I argue in the closing chapter, even these predictions may well underestimate the unfolding electoral impacts of the outrage North Carolinians now demonstrate across all 100 counties over the assaults that President Donald Trump, NC Senate leader Phil Berger, and Paul Newby have lodged against the foundations of our government and the decencies of our society.

But, of course, if Democrats come to control even one house of the General Assembly, Republicans will likely prove far more willing to vote to repair the system. And taking away the power of politicians to create their own districts is immensely popular both in North Carolina and around the country. Democrats should be clear, in fact more than clear, that resecuring constitutional democracy by removing districting abuse from the prerogative of the General Assembly is at the core of all Democratic Party campaigns across the state of North Carolina. Democrats, it is perhaps redundant to say, are existentially committed to democracy. And they will remain committed to democracy when they return to power.

In 2025, state representatives Pricey Harrison, Marcia Morey, and Robert Reives (all Democrats) introduced House Bill 20, or the Fair Maps Act. Its summary reveals its essential purpose: "An Act to Amend the North Carolina Constitution to Provide for an Independent Redistricting Process, to Establish the North Carolina Citizens Redistricting Committee." The proposal was immediately dispatched to a quick death in the rules committee by Republican leaders—no surprise there.

It might be more surprising to learn that Phil Berger and former Speaker of the NC House of Representatives Tim Moore favored the creation of an independent districting commission years ago, when they and their fellow Republicans were in the minority in the General Assembly—now, apparently, not so much.

Reportedly, the first attempt to set up an independent redistricting process in North Carolina occurred in 2013 with House Bill 606. It passed the Republican-controlled House of Representatives by an amazing 82–28 vote. What was equally surprising was that Thom Tillis was the House Speaker then. But the proposal died, without a vote, in the state senate.

The first version of the Fair Maps Act was introduced a decade earlier by State Representative Reives, who is currently the Democratic NC House minority leader. It was, of course, quickly scuttled by a more seasoned and boldly entrenched set of Republican leaders. The 2025 successor was modeled after a similar commission that was approved by California voters in 2008. It would have been comprised of fifteen members: five Democrats, five Republicans, and five folks who are unaffiliated with either major party. No lawmakers, lobbyists, major political donors, or relatives of legislators would have been allowed to serve. The commission would have been required to hold at least twenty-five public meetings: at least ten before drawing new district maps and another ten before any plans were finalized. Approval of the final maps would have required at least nine well-distributed votes: three or more from each of the disparate membership groups. If the commission were unable to secure the prescribed threshold, a special master would be appointed to complete the task. Districts would have been required to be equal in population, contiguous, compact, and compliant with federal law with a limit on the splitting of counties, municipalities, and communities of interest. Neither the General Assembly nor the state supreme court would have been part of the enacting process.

National experts have noted, to our shame, that North Carolina is the most heavily gerrymandered state in the union—the state with the most profoundly biased system. That actually means, in operation, that we are the least democratic state in the country, the most rejectionist of the promise of the Declaration of Independence, the least committed to the American experiment. I'm confident that we won't continue to tolerate it.

## CHAPTER FOUR

★ ★ ★

# Administering Justice
# "Without Favoritism to Anyone"

n chapter 2, I briefly described the North Carolina Supreme Court's remarkable abdication of its obligations of independent judicial review. Rather than enforcing the constitutional guardrails that are referred to in the justices' oath of office, the new Republican court has declared its undying fealty to the "great and chief department of government" in North Carolina—the (Republican) General Assembly—which "represents the sacrosanct fulfillment of the people's will." Accordingly, a bold green light has been lit before our state's greedy and lawless legislators, threatening to end limited government and constitutionally constrained democracy as it has been understood in North Carolina for generations.

But there is more.

Deference hasn't been the North Carolina high court's only sin. The court's Republican majority, or at least four of them, have begun to directly intervene in the state's electoral process—picking

winners and losers, rejecting and directly thwarting, or even over-
turning, the will of the voters—in ways that have almost never
occurred in the United States and that have shocked both the
state and the nation. I'll describe briefly how that has come to
pass and outline steps that could be taken to combat it.

Small steps of direct judicial interference with elections began
with *Kennedy v. North Carolina State Board of Elections* in October 2024, just before that year's presidential election. Robert F.
Kennedy Jr. had fought hard to get on the ballot in North Carolina, starting a political party named the We the People Party to
ease the process. The state board had certified Kennedy's group
as a party, and he had been placed on the ballot as its nominee.
When Kennedy suspended his campaign and endorsed former
(and now current) President Donald Trump, he belatedly sought
to be removed from the ballot in North Carolina—after taking
contradictory stances, in various states, about whether he re-
mained a candidate. Counties had already begun printing ballots with Kennedy's name at the time that he withdrew in late
August.

Following state law, the Board of Elections denied Kennedy's
request. Almost three million ballots had already been printed, absentee timelines would have been delayed, and new ballots would
have been printed and paid for by 100 North Carolina county
election boards, not the state, costing $1 million or more. Appar-
ently fearing that Kennedy's presence on the ballot might weaken
Trump's prospects in a close North Carolina election, a 4–3 Republican NC Supreme Court majority ditched the election

board's determination and ordered that new ballots be printed despite the cost—and the resulting delay in mailing absentee ballots to Tar Heels who had requested them.

Justice Trey Allen, writing for the majority, fretted that people mistakenly voting for Kennedy would be disenfranchised:

> We acknowledge that expediting the process of printing new ballots will require considerable time and effort by our election officials and significant expense to the State. But that is a price the North Carolina Constitution expects us to incur to protect voters' fundamental right to vote and have their vote count.

Surprise, surprise. Who would have guessed that the new Republican NC Supreme Court had any interest in citizens' "right to vote and have their vote count" following the cascade of decisions that had been handed down just months earlier embracing extreme partisan gerrymandering, disenfranchising people who have been convicted of felonies, and embracing race-based voter identification requirements?

Justice Allison Riggs objected in dissent, writing that the ruling placed "the whims of one man above the constitutional interests of tens of thousands of voters [facing] an effectively truncated absentee period." The "egregious interference with the electoral process represented a dark day in the history of the state's judiciary." She added that "public aspersions cast on the impartiality, independence and dignity of our state courts are well earned."

In a sense, though, another dissent was even more compelling.

The RFK Jr. ruling was 4–3, not the traditional 5–2 Republican lineup. Republican Justice Richard Dietz, for the first time, departed from his hyperpartisan colleagues. He concluded the following in his separate dissent: "I believe this Court's role is to follow the law as it is written. The State Board of Elections properly determined that it would not be practical to reprint the ballots before the deadline set by law. Our election laws permitted the Board to decline to reprint the ballots."

You wouldn't think that Justice Dietz's words would have set him starkly apart. But they did. Until that moment, he had played the loyal Republican foot soldier. Justice Dietz had been an actual judge before he was elected to the state's high court. It was like his muscle memory kicked in, at least for the moment, saying implicitly to his fellow Republican adventurists, *I'm basically with you folks, but still, I'm a judge. There's just no law supporting your political interventions here. I'm on your side, but there's got to be a limit. This is way past it.*

It turns out that Justice Dietz was right to be wary.

In February 2023, after the new Republican NC Supreme Court assumed power, after Justice Philip Berger Jr. bragged in an official opinion of a news story touting "a lasting Republican grip on the Supreme Court," and after the new majority issued what the *New York Times* called "an extraordinary pair of orders" requiring re-hearings in two major voting rights cases that had been decided only seven weeks earlier, I wrote an essay for the *Raleigh News & Observer* and the *Charlotte Observer* titled, "Welcome to What Will Quickly Become the Most Partisan

Court in NC History." It turns out that I understated. Even as cynical as I might have become, I would never have assumed that the North Carolina Supreme Court's Republican justices would try to overtly, illegally, patently, and corruptly steal an election to defeat one of their colleagues and seat one of their friends. I thought they were villainous. But I didn't think they would do that, not in the United States. It was simply too far outside the norms of the legal profession and the operations of US democracy. Apparently, this was not so.

Judge Jefferson Griffin, who sits (still) on the North Carolina Court of Appeals, faced Democratic incumbent Allison Riggs in the November 2024 election for a seat on the NC Supreme Court. Justice Riggs was declared the winner of the race by an exceptionally slim margin, 734 votes. Judge Griffin, unsurprisingly, sought a recount—twice. When those failed, he filed a protest with the NC State Board of Elections.

Judge Griffin wanted the ballots of roughly 65,000 voters to be invalidated. Mostly, he said that they were ineligible to vote because certain personal data hadn't been recorded when they registered. The omissions, he admitted, weren't the voters' faults but were because of administrative errors in the registration process. The objection was also artificial because the voters had been required to show identification when they voted. Still, he pressed on. The election board rejected Judge Griffin's claim.

Judge Griffin then raced to the North Carolina Supreme Court, where his friends were, for review. The case shifted back and forth between the state and federal systems. But the North

Carolina Supreme Court intervened twice without justification or conceivable legal basis: first blocking Justice Riggs's election from being certified and later invalidating an array of votes that were likely sufficient to overthrow the results of the election and install Judge Griffin. Adopting a position that had never before been recognized in US law, the NC Supreme Court's Republican majority acted to invalidate votes that had been legally cast according to the rules that were in place on the day of the election, to give Judge Griffin what he wanted. Finally, then, the federal courts had enough. Judge Richard Myers II, chief judge of the US District Court for the Eastern District of North Carolina and a Trump appointee, stepped in to stop the steal. Judge Myers concluded, to the surprise of none, that the retroactive invalidation of ballots that was ordered by the North Carolina Supreme Court was a rank violation of the United States Constitution. Judge Myers wrote, barely shielding his outrage, as follows:

> This case [asks] whether the federal constitution permits a state to alter the rules of an election after the fact and apply those changes retroactively to only a select group of voters.
>
> The answer is "no." The principle that the legal effect of conduct should ordinarily be assessed under the law that exists when the conduct took place has timeless and universal human appeal. That principle will be familiar to anyone who has played a sport or a board game. You establish the rules before the game. You don't change them after the game is done.

Judge Myers ordered that the North Carolina Supreme Court's shocking and illegitimate decision be blocked. He commanded that Justice Riggs's successful election be certified. On May 13, 2025, six months after the election was held, Justice Allison Riggs was sworn in for an eight-year term. Massive protests in every corner of North Carolina demonstrating against the state supreme court's stunning effort to literally overthrow democracy in the Tar Heel State were converted to celebrations. Theft, apparently, has its limits.

The North Carolina Supreme Court rulings blocking the certification and then attempting to overturn the Griffin–Riggs election were, once again, not 5–2 sweeps. Justice Dietz, in an inspiring display of political courage, dissented from his Republican colleagues' pathbreaking illegality. One fears, in North Carolina, that Justice Dietz will never again receive the nomination of his party. Honest judicial decision-making is literally disqualifying in the North Carolina Republican Party.

It is hard to believe that the straightforward, universal, legal principles that were announced by Judge Myers were beyond the comprehension of Paul Newby, Philip Berger Jr., Tamara Barringer, and Trey Allen—the Republican justices who attempted to use all the power they could muster to pilfer Riggs's election. What was missing was the belief that they were required to comply with rules at all. They didn't make a mistake. They aren't stupid. They acted with cold calculation to fraudulently and corruptly abuse their powers. They willfully violated the state constitution and their oaths of office. Their own colleague, Justice Dietz, had obviously tried to explain their illegality to them. It didn't matter. They aren't actually judges, just partisan hucksters, political operatives out to override democracy in the Tar Heel State. That's what we have. As my mother-in-law used to say, "It is what it is."

And the pattern continues.

As I mentioned in chapter 2, in early 2025, the General Assembly passed an extraordinary law, again not previously seen in the United States, shifting the governor's power to appoint members of the state election commission to the state auditor, who was a newly elected Republican named David Boliek. Governor Josh Stein, of course, immediately sued to challenge the constitutionality of the act. And just as unsurprisingly, a Raleigh three-judge court quickly ruled that the power-stripping measure violated foundational notions of the separation of powers.

"Because the duty to faithfully execute the laws has been exclusively assigned to the governor, Senate Bill 382 cannot reassign that duty to the auditor without violating the Constitution," the judges concluded.

High school civics stuff.

A week later, though, a three-judge NC Court of Appeals panel issued a one-page order allowing the statute to go into effect despite the ruling. The appellate judges, the *Raleigh News & Observer* reported, "didn't reveal their names, hear oral arguments, or provide a rationale" for their decision. No emergency was identified or existent. Oddly, the decree didn't maintain the status quo, it upset it, allowing a declared-invalid law to go into effect without inquiry. Governor Stein quickly appealed the decision to the North Carolina Supreme Court, seeking an immediate administrative stay to block the unusual order. He argued, "Today's Court of Appeals decision about the Board of Elections poses a threat to our democracy and the rule of law; the Supreme Court should not allow it to stand."

Despite intervening repeatedly in Judge Griffin's case in violation of traditional appellate norms, after receiving Governor Stein's petition, the North Carolina Supreme Court went into an unfamiliar radio silence. Mum was the word. As a result, Boliek was free to reconstitute the state election commission. In his 2024 campaign, Boliek said that it's really important to know "that I understand that as state auditor you have to leave party politics at the door." It turns out that he wasn't telling the truth.

After keeping one incumbent Republican member on the board, Boliek chose two of the most wildly partisan Republicans ever to live in North Carolina. Bob Rucho, who astonished the nation and the United States Supreme Court itself with his extreme partisan gerrymandering practices while in the state legislature, and Francis De Luca, a former Republican congressional candidate and the president of the right-wing Civitas Institute were seated (apparently, Art Pope was busy). The board's new Republican majority then fired the commission's executive director, Karen Brinson Bell, an experienced and well-regarded administrator who was also the incoming president of the National Association of State Election Directors. A new sheriff was in town—just in time.

Katelin Kaiser, policy director of Democracy North Carolina, was not stunned by the unexplained behavior of the NC Court of Appeals and the North Carolina Supreme Court: "This version of the court has shown us time and time again that it is not following the law for the people but for the political party."

Eventually, the Republican majority upheld the NC Court of Appeals order. Justice Riggs dissented, arguing that the court was "rewriting precedent and creating an explanation for an unexplained Court of Appeals order to upend a 125-year status quo for the North Carolina State Board of Elections." Justice Anita Earls was more candid, in words the Republican majority again made no effort to rebut:

> If the voters of North Carolina wanted a Republican to control the State Board of Elections, they could have elected a Republican governor. If they wanted David Boliek (the Auditor) in particular to run our elections, they could have elected him governor. The voters did not. They hired Joshua Stein and David Boliek to do specific jobs, and the General Assembly is restructuring those jobs after the election. The General Assembly may not grab power over enforcement of election laws by shuttling the Board between statewide elected officials until it finds one willing to do its bidding.

## "Without Favoritism to Anyone"

One notable benefit has occurred as a result of Judge Griffin's fraudulent odyssey. North Carolinians are now terrified by their own state supreme court. They understand that the law doesn't matter to these folks. And now it has been proven, right before everyone's eyes, that no transgression is beyond their venality. So, in one sense, the remedy for such judicial authoritarianism will likely occur, eventually, through the political process. Ironically, Justices Newby, Berger, Barringer, and Allen have shown themselves to be so politically corrupted that they are likely now unelectable. It is hard to imagine anyone winning reelection in North Carolina with the Jefferson Griffin votes hanging from their necks. Even potential tyrants sometimes overplay their hands.

It is also essential that the North Carolina Bar Association cast aside its timidity and publicly condemn the partisan actions of the North Carolina Supreme Court. Incalculable damage to democracy, to the rule of law, and to the North Carolina Supreme Court as an institution has been inflicted. The bar can't continue to shield its eyes. The wounds will last for decades. Recovery begins with the admission of over-the-top transgression. This has yet to occur.

When Justice Riggs was belatedly sworn in to her new eight-year term, she swore an oath of office like other members of the state supreme court before her. She "solemnly" promised, of course, to "support the Constitution of the United States" and to "support, maintain, and defend" the North Carolina State Constitution. She also swore explicitly "to administer justice without favoritism to anyone." By now, I don't think any lawyer or engaged citizen of North Carolina believes that Justices Newby, Berger, Barringer, and Allen administer justice without favoritism to anyone. We are a deeply polarized state, so I concede that a lot of Tar Heel Republicans likely support what these four Republican "judges" are doing. But no honest human would argue that they adjudicate without favoritism. They've settled on their course.

Some will recall that in 1996, the General Assembly changed superior court elections from partisan to nonpartisan in North Carolina. In 2002, the legislature also converted district court and appellate judicial races to nonpartisan status. As part of the switch, in 2004, the legislature provided public funding for appellate judicial candidates who agree to spending limits for their campaigns. In 2013, with the Republican takeover of the General Assembly, public funding was ended. Partisan appellate judicial elections were then reinstituted in 2018. Republicans in North Carolina are obviously committed to expensive, partisan judicial races.

I wish we could return to the nonpartisan, publicly funded judges' elections of yore. And some strong Democratic members of the General Assembly advocate for exactly that. But, to be candid, I'm inclined to think that with the unlimited independent expenditures that are now protected and massively practiced by both parties and their supporters as a result of the unfortunate decision reached in *Citizens United v. Federal Election Commission*, it may, practically speaking, be too late to go back to that earlier, less dangerous ground.

So if conscience, censure, and protest can't force justices Newby, Berger, Barringer, and Allen to resign, then the only way that a system of equal justice can return to the Tar Heel State is through a deeply invigorated commitment by the Democratic Party to appellate judicial races, especially those of the North Carolina Supreme Court. And, given existing terms, a successful and complete judicial revolution is likely not possible until 2028. The good news, or at least the better news, is that a pathway to resuscitating the broken Tar Heel judicial system is clear even if it is longer in duration than North Carolinians likely prefer.

The next NC Supreme Court race will occur in 2026, when Justice Earls will seek to retain her seat. Justice Earls is likely the most accomplished jurist ever to sit on the North Carolina Supreme Court. She is an internationally recognized human rights scholar, and her judicial record on the high court has matched that singular reputation. She has also proven to be a staunch and fearless opponent of the lawlessness, political corruption, and unprofessionalism of the Republican NC Supreme Court. The quality of her opinions both annoys and humiliates the weak and tepid, unlawyerly offerings of justices Newby, Berger, and the like. The fact that she is the only Black member of the high court, and repeatedly calls out the racialized transgressions of her Republican colleagues, seems to drive her partisan opponents to frenzy. They have, therefore, threatened her with impeachment and sought to have her sanctioned by the NC Judicial Standards Commission for uttering clearly constitutionally protected speech, positions that would embarrass any actual lawyer. She is also one of the most committed political candidates to honor the state with her service. The long saga of Judge Griffin's effort to pilfer a state supreme court seat has notably lifted North Carolinians' understanding of both the importance of judicial elections and the ruthlessness of Republican partisans. The only announced Republican opponent of Justice Earls at the time of this writing is State Rep. Sarah Stevens, a nine-term Republican member of the General Assembly whose legislative record reveals her to be an extremist on racial and political gerrymandering issues as well as vouchers for religious schools. Like other North Carolina Republican lawmakers, she has a track record of constitutional transgressions that is almost unmatched in the nation. And whether the Republican nominee is State Representative Stevens or some other person, her candidacy again reveals the working assumption that state supreme court seats are political rather than legal positions. It is, in short, impossible to imagine a greater judicial mismatch on the merits. And, without a doubt, Justice Earls's re-election will be the most important race on the state ballot in 2026.

However, high noon for the North Carolina justice system, the mother of all state supreme court elections, will occur in 2028. Republican justices Newby, Berger, and Barringer will, one assumes, seek re-election. Justice Newby is, of course, the most potently partisan chief justice in North Carolina history; he is the main architect of the state supreme court's destruction. Justice Berger mocks the entire legal enterprise of the state by refusing to recuse himself from cases in which his father is a party. There's no appearance of partiality there, of course. And Justice Barringer took the most extreme position, among extreme positions, in the

Griffin case. She argued for suspending all procedural standards to immediately give Judge Griffin the result he wanted. These three are the high priests of North Carolina political corruption. And their Democratic opponents will be charged with letting the entire state know it—chapter and horrifying verse.

Some structural changes should help as well. If Democrats have undervalued judicial elections in the past, those days are likely gone. North Carolina Democratic Party Chair Anderson Clayton has, for the first time, created a coordinated campaign that focuses exclusively on judicial races, recognizing that "extreme Republicans have wielded judicial power to bend the knee to anything the state legislature wants." To that end, in May 2025, Democrats launched Unite For Justice rallies across the state, featuring not only Justice Earls, but judges of all levels, with Clayton explaining that Tar Heels "are fed up with what Republicans are doing and aren't going to stand for it." Enthusiasm was fueled by the lessons and engagement of Justice Riggs's campaign. It is a welcome change.

Justice Riggs also spoke more openly in her campaign about crucial, substantive issues like voting rights and reproductive freedom, following the pattern of successful state supreme court elections the year earlier in Wisconsin. Duke University Professor Asher Hildebrand noted that with "increasingly partisan judicial elections," when justices or candidates "embrace that fact, voters respond favorably to it." Republicans, of course, attempted to misuse North Carolina Judicial Standards Commission proceedings against Justice Riggs, as they had earlier with Justice

Earls. But our opportunity for justice lies with empowered judicial elections, and with elections come ideas, and with ideas
comes the First Amendment. Republican judicial candidates and
their consultants likely prefer an electoral landscape where no
candidates can speak of voting rights or abortions before they as-
cend to the high courts to deny electoral freedom and reproductive liberties. Still, that's not democracy, and as we've now learned
in the Tar Heel State, it's not the rule of law.

But most importantly, Tar Heel voters now recognize, patently, that their freedom and their constitutional democracy will
be placed squarely on the ballot in the 2028 state supreme court
elections. Justices Newby, Berger, and Barringer are out to destroy
them. They've proved it repeatedly. At least two of the three Republican incumbents must be defeated in 2028 if democracy is to
prevail in North Carolina. As Clayton has explained, "We have
to get involved with the courts because courts are about freedom
and fairness and opportunity." Without them, in North Carolina, the rest is lost.

## CHAPTER FIVE

★ ★ ★

# A Right to Equal Dignity and Full Membership

O f course, denying the right to participate equally in the political process is not the only way to restrict one's full citizenship and one's claim to equal dignity and worth. North Carolina's Republican General Assembly has developed other specialties as well.

In 2022, the United States Supreme Court handed down a ruling in *Dobbs v. Jackson Women's Health Organization* that overturned *Roe v. Wade* and fifty years of federal constitutional protection for abortion rights. In an opinion by Justice Samuel Alito Jr. that was both angry and defensive, the court concluded that no state abortion regulations could be held to violate the US Constitution, no matter how extreme the provision might be. Laws providing no exceptions for rape, incest, or grave danger to a person's health, for example, were deemed nonproblematic. Anyone who could get pregnant no longer enjoyed the constitutional right to reproductive freedom in the United States.

Justice Alito employed a rigid theory of originalist interpretation that has been violated regularly and pervasively by the high court for generations or even centuries. For Alito, if a constitutional ruling was not deeply rooted in the text and history of the provision upon which it was based, the original understanding of its enactors, then the judgment was illegitimate. *No text, no history, no law*, the claim goes. But Justice Alito's originalism, in operation, is only applied to restrict the claims of his adversaries — to own the libs. He has felt free to ignore his own rule at will when it suits his politics. A few months after the *Dobbs* decision, the justices declared racial affirmative action unconstitutional under the Fourteenth Amendment despite the fact that the Reconstruction-era Congress that proposed the amendment practiced race-based affirmative action routinely, believing it to further the egalitarian purposes of the equal protection clause rather than thwarting them. In *Students for Fair Admissions v. Harvard*, throwing out the University of North Carolina at Chapel Hill admissions program, originalism was apparently deemed to be only a rule for suckers. Alito and his friends simply ignored the deep principles that they had previously announced in *Dobbs*. Constraining theories of interpretation bar only the aspirations of their opponents. And, the next summer, the US Supreme Court announced the most nonoriginalist opinion in its history in the Donald Trump immunity case. Ruling that the president of the United States was no longer subject to criminal prosecution, the Republican justices violated the Constitution's text, legislative history, the statements of the framers, the understanding of all past presidents, and 235 years of settled judicial precedent. The Roberts–Trump–Alito Court is not dominated by straight shooters.

The *Dobbs* decision was dishonest in a second, more direct way. Justice Alito's originalist theory obviously endangered an array of other high-visibility, personal-autonomy rulings. Cases like *Griswold v. Connecticut* (the right to use contraceptives), *Loving v. Virginia* (the right to marry someone of a different race), *Lawrence v. Texas* (the right to be free from criminal prosecution for private, adult, consensual sexual activity), and *Obergefell v. Hodges* (the right to marry someone of the same sex) cannot be squared with the court's theory in *Dobbs*. Justice Clarence Thomas even wrote separately to urge that all these privacy cornerstones should be dispatched with *Roe*. But Alito was adamant, somewhat ironically, that he wrote a rule that was applicable only to abortion cases—as if that could justify and relieve the purported anxieties of those who opposed the controversial ruling. "It is hard to see how we could be clearer," Alito thundered. *Shut up and take my word for it*, he seemed to say, hoping that we'd all forget that in his confirmation hearings, he'd declared that *Roe v. Wade*, for him, was settled Supreme Court precedent.

Here, Justice Brent Kavanaugh piped in, saying he "emphasize[d] what the Court today states: Overruling *Roe* does not mean the overruling of those precedents and does not threaten or cast doubt on those precedents." He took annoyed umbrage at such a suggestion, especially given Justice Alito's declamations. *Don't believe your lying eyes*, Kavanaugh effectively cracked. He was perhaps hoping that we had all forgotten that he himself had testified before the US Senate Committee on the Judiciary: "*Roe v. Wade* is settled precedent of the Supreme Court. One of the most important things to keep in mind about *Roe* is that it has been confirmed many times over the past 45 years—most pointedly in *Carey v. Population Services*. It is precedent on precedent."

Then, of course, Justice Kavanaugh overturned *Roe* the first chance he got, showing himself to be a Trump justice in all the ways that matter, including, especially, lying. The fundamental human rights of millions, or eventually hundreds of millions, were not enough to merit his candor. And the dishonest Roberts Court ideology, which allows the purported religious beliefs of a minority of Americans to defeat the full dignity and citizenship of people across the land, carries potent impacts on the quality of life and community in North Carolina.

In May 2023, the North Carolina General Assembly accepted the United States Supreme Court's invitation to limit fifty years of reproductive freedom. Senate Bill 20 was passed along party lines, overriding then-Governor Roy Cooper's pointed veto. Broadly speaking, the statute bans abortion in North Carolina after the first twelve weeks of pregnancy. In cases of rape or incest, abortion is allowed through the twentieth week. And if a "life-limiting" fetal abnormality is documented, abortion is legal until the twenty-fourth week. Those seeking abortions must undergo a seventy-two-hour waiting period and an in-person, biased counseling session. The waiting period is among the longest in the nation and necessitates two clinic visits. The statute also requires a follow-up doctor's office visitation seven to fourteen days after a medication abortion. Abortions performed under one of the statute's exceptions must occur in a hospital. Additional medically unnecessary regulations for abortion clinics and facilities reduce access to reproductive health care statewide, particularly for rural and low-income people, of course.

In 1992, US Supreme Court Justice Sandra Day O'Connor, the high tribunal's first female member, wrote in *Planned Parenthood of Southeastern Pennsylvania v. Casey*:

Our law affords constitutional protection to personal decisions relating to marriage, procreation, contraception, family relationships, childrearing, and education.... These matters, involving the most intimate and personal choices a person may make in a lifetime, choices central to personal dignity and autonomy, are central to the liberty protected by the Fourteenth Amendment. At the heart of liberty is the right to define one's own concept of existence, of meaning, of the universe, and the mystery of human life. Beliefs about these matters could not define the attributes of personhood were they formed under the compulsion of the state. [A woman's] suffering is too intimate and personal for the state to insist, without more, upon its own vision of the woman's role, however dominant that vision has been in the course of our history and our culture. The destiny of the woman must be shaped...on her own conception of her spiritual imperatives and her place in society.... Women's ability to participate equally in the economic and social life of the Nation has been facilitated by their ability to control their reproductive lives.

North Carolina's abortion law (SB 20) was not, it goes without saying, the most restrictive in the country. It is, however, radically inconsistent with the vision of constitutive liberty described so powerfully by Justice O'Connor in *Casey*. A state abortion ban, of course, directly interferes with the "most intimate and personal choices" that "a person may make in a lifetime." Choices that are "central to dignity and autonomy" should be ensured freedoms. The North Carolina statute specifically deploys waiting periods and abortion facility regulations that serve no medical purpose. Their obvious goal, instead, is to make it more difficult, more burdensome, and more costly to secure reproductive care, especially for people without significant economic resources and work flexibility. SB 20 curtails North Carolinians' ability to define, and carry forward, their "own concept of existence, of meaning, of the mystery of human life" under "the compulsion of the state." It violates Justice O'Connor's declaration that an abortion decision is "too intimate for the state to insist upon its own vision of the woman's role, however dominant that vision has been in the course of our history and cultures." It, undoubtedly, surrenders a person's "own concepts of spiritual imperative" in favor of the religious beliefs of third parties—politically powerful third parties. And it constrains people's "ability to control their reproductive lives" and, as a result, denies the "ability to participate equally in the economic and social life of the Nation." Neither strangers, nor the government, should be understood to have the power to inflict such wounds on a fellow human being, no matter how enthusiastically or sanctimoniously they wish to do so.

Nor, just as clearly, should they be allowed to enforce such restrictions on "central" components of liberty and equality when the majority of the citizenry is decidedly opposed to it. Broadly speaking, more than 60 percent of Tar Heels, and the country overall, support access to abortion rights free of coercion by the state. Polls indicate, more particularly, that North Carolina voters oppose SB 20 and its twelve-week abortion ban by double-digit margins. Republicans understand this well, which is why they have fought to keep abortion issues off the ballot, as has successfully occurred in so many other states. Members of the General Assembly, and their patrons on the North Carolina Supreme Court, claim routinely that the legislature is "the great and chief department of government," representing the "sacrosanct fulfillment of the people's will." But when it comes to abortion rights, they want to stay as far away from the "will of the people" as is humanly possible. Lawmakers are happier to exercise their disproportionate authorities, achieved through extreme gerrymanders, on behalf of a politicized, purportedly religious minority of Tar Heels who are determined to impose their predispositions on everyone else. They no doubt believe their political backers' preferences count more robustly, more deservingly, and more permanently than those of the rest of us. Democracy and constitutionalism be damned.

North Carolina progressives, it is perhaps too obvious to state, must successfully repeal SB 20. They should replace it with a statute codifying the long-settled protections of *Roe v. Wade*, securing a person's right to terminate a pregnancy until the fetus is viable. It is profoundly unacceptable to North Carolinians that our daughters, today, enjoy dramatically diminished reproductive freedoms compared to their mothers and grandmothers. Tar Heels are unwilling to surrender their most intimate liberties to the purportedly religious demands of politicians and their fevered followers. Those good folks should be content to run their own houses.

And it is perhaps equally clear that North Carolinians should permanently remove the scope of reproductive freedom from the endless vagaries of political machination. Even with SB 20 on the books, Republican leaders suggest bolder repressive ambitions. US Rep. (then–NC House Speaker) Tim Moore has expressed interest in enacting a six-week ban to more effectively close off a person's right to choose. In the 2024 election, Hal Weatherman, the Republican nominee for lieutenant governor, ran on a "heartbeat bill" proposal and gubernatorial candidate Mark Robinson boasted of being able to deliver a complete abortion prohibition in the state. During the 2025 session, Republican stalwarts introduced an abortion ban with the only exception being to save the life of the mother. It included felony criminal charges and a $100,000 minimum fine for transgressors. It didn't pass. But, for such folks, extremism is the only order of the day. And North Carolinians have repeatedly seen the impossible become the possible and then the law. It's essential, therefore, to write abortion rights into the North Carolina State Constitution.

In May 2024, Democratic State Senator Rachel Hunt (who is now the lieutenant governor) introduced Senate Bill 909, the Protect Women's Healthcare amendment, which would amend Article I of the state constitution to protect abortion access. Her proposal carried the endorsement, or co-sponsorship, of an array of Democratic state senators (Val Applewhite, Julie Mayfield, Graig Meyer, Gladys Robinson, DeAndrea Salvador, and Kandie Smith). Its terms were straightforward and ambitious:

> The State shall not restrict a woman's right to decide to have an abortion. Additionally, the State shall not restrict access to contraception, fertility treatment, continuing one's own pregnancy, or miscarriage care. The State may restrict the ability of a woman to choose whether or not to terminate a pregnancy after fetal viability, unless such a termination is necessary to preserve the life or health of the woman.

Arizona passed a similar constitutional provision by wide margins in 2024. Its preamble puts the issue well:

> Arizonans believe strongly in individual autonomy. Which includes the right of each individual to make personal decisions about their own health care without overbearing and unnecessary government interference. When the United States Supreme Court overturned *Roe v. Wade* and deprived Arizonans of their longstanding right to abortion, Arizonans' autonomy over their own health care was immediately threatened. To protect Arizonans' rights and ensure access to reproductive health care, the Constitution must be

amended to establish a fundamental right to abortion. This act should be liberally construed in furtherance of the fundamental right it establishes.

Since the *Dobbs* decision, similar amending measures have been passed by the people of Colorado, Maryland, Missouri, Montana, Nevada, New York, California, Michigan, Ohio, and Vermont.

Of course, to no one's surprise, the Republican leadership of the North Carolina General Assembly immediately dispatched SB 909 to an unceremonious death in the Rules Committee. Literally the last thing on earth our Republicans want to learn is their constituents' opinions on abortion. When pressed, they cover their ears. They take their marching orders from religious extremists who are certain that they have the right to run other people's lives. *Don't upset us with the facts, or with your liberties*, they effectively say. *The majority doesn't rule here; white evangelicals do*. And recall, as Mark Twain put it, "Nothing so needs reforming as other people's habits."

But North Carolinians have less trust in these folks each passing week. We've grown tired of their efforts to demean our democracy and crush our liberties with their suggested claims of superiority. The demand to run our own lives and our own government rises. It's not going to recede. The right to reproductive freedom *is* going to be protected in North Carolina. It's not hard to discern what the actual Republican position on this is: *We'll just fly to New York to get our abortions. And if you can't afford to fly to New York, then you don't matter*. But that won't be

North Carolina's rule, no matter how much our would-be-bosses demand it.

## "North Carolinians' Fundamental Right to Privacy Shall Not Be Denied"

Sadly, reproductive freedoms are not the only privacy rights that are under constant threat in North Carolina. As I indicated in the early pages of this chapter, the right to use contraceptives, the right to engage in sexual intimacy, the right to marry someone of the same sex, and the like have long been based on federally protected constitutional rights to privacy. Justices Alito and Kavanaugh, of course, swore to continue ensuring such liberties in the *Dobbs* decision. But they are liars. It is unfathomable to me that any Tar Heel would rely on their assertions. And the North Carolina Republican General Assembly has a long, pioneering record of trying to interfere with what Justice O'Connor described as "the most intimate and personal choices a person may make in a lifetime." They are eager to do it again. And our politicized state supreme court will, unfortunately, only urge them on.

In 2012, North Carolina became the last state in the country to prohibit same-sex marriage. After the *Obergefell* decision invalidated North Carolina's marriage-ban amendment, our Republican lawmakers became more inventive. In 2015, Senator Phil Berger pushed through a law allowing registrars and magistrates to refuse to issue marriage licenses to any couple whom the public officials had "a sincerely held religious objection" to serving. As a result, a

stoutly believing North Carolina magistrate doesn't have to per-
form their statutory duty if they don't like the gay, lesbian, bisex-
ual, or transgender persons in front of them—nor, for that matter,
the mixed-race couple or the Muslim couple seeking a license. Our
magistrates are allowed to value their supposedly religious predispositions more highly than their constitutionally sworn duties to
provide equal protection under the law. Allegedly Christian magistrates get special exemptions to violate the constitutional guarantees of those they despise. Republican former State Rep. Larry
Pittman explained, "State employees should not be required to
sanction something they consider perverted." We thus have, now,
two classes of public officials in North Carolina: fundamentalist
Christians for whom constitutional mandates are voluntary and
everyone else, to whom the rules apply.

More famously, in 2016, North Carolina Republicans passed
the internationally notorious House Bill 2, or the "bathroom bill."
We thus became the first state in the country to require transgender persons to use the public bathrooms and locker rooms of the
gender on their birth certificates. As Maxine Eichner, a sex discrimination scholar at UNC–Chapel Hill, put it, "No one had
ever done this." The *New York Times* decreed that North Carolina led the nation in bigotry. National, and even international,
protests erupted. Boycotts cost the state thousands of jobs and
billions of dollars. The *Greensboro News & Record* bemoaned
that it was "painfully obvious" that "official state policy is hostile
to the gay and transgender community." The *Asheville Citizen
Times* wrote that "Carolina now equates the LGBT community

with child molesters." The United States government sued North Carolina for targeting the most vulnerable of its own people.

Apparently most ominously of all, North Carolina lost out on the NBA All-Star Game and the NCAA threatened to make North Carolina ineligible to host basketball tournaments for six years. Some wounds are too great to be borne. So, in May 2017, the Republican leadership of the General Assembly agreed to a partial repeal of HB 2, eliminating the bathroom-birth-certificate requirement but preventing cities from regulating bathroom use until 2020. *The Guardian* labeled the substitute "cruel and insulting." Still, it ended most of the public uproar.

So, why reprise old wounds? In late March 2025, a group of Republican state senators introduced Senate Bill 516, the Women's Safety and Protection Act. It would bar trans people from using unisex restrooms, changing facilities, and sleeping quarters that correspond to their gender identities. The scope of the new bill is less encompassing than its predecessor, applying to schools, prisons, confinement facilities, and domestic violence and rape crisis centers. But the applicability to shelters is additionally threatening, with lawmakers perhaps hoping to open transgender abuse victims to further torment. And the purported rationale—protecting women from assault at the hands of transgender assailants— remains as patently false as it ever was. The provision would also define "male" and "female" in state law strictly according to sex assigned at birth and prohibit the alteration of sex markers on birth certificates and driver's licenses.

The new bathroom bill seems to enjoy ample Republican support. It was sponsored by Republican state senators Vickie Saw-yer and Brad Overcash and includes an array of co-sponsors, in-cluding powerful leadership member Ralph Hise Jr., and State Senator Berger says he's "considering it," noting, "We always want to do as much as possible to protect women and girls." Berger also pointed out that, these days, "Similar legislation has been filed in other states." So, reading between the lines, Republicans might be able to get away with humiliating trans people without the entire planet erupting like it did nine years ago. The prospects, therefore, might be deemed too exciting to resist.

And Bathroom Bill 2.0 appears amidst a massive national Re-publican wave of antitransgender statutes and regulations. Most famously, perhaps, Trump's cruel and defamatory executive or-der purports to remove all transgender people from the armed forces. North Carolina banned gender-affirming care for minors and barred trans athletes from participating in women's sports in 2023.

Democratic former State Rep. John Autry argued passion-ately against the care ban, discussing the challenges faced by his twenty-one-year-old granddaughter. "Using children as a politi-cal football simply to engage your voters is despicable and be-neath the North Carolina General Assembly." The "legislature has no purpose getting between medical professionals and a fam-ily." He reported that after he spoke on the statehouse floor, he received a voicemail saying, "Cry more, groomer."

He asked, "How despicable do you have to be to say that to

someone who is speaking in defense of their grandchild? Maybe the cruelty is the point."

I understand, of course, that Republicans, especially the current president of the United States, successfully demagogued animosity against transgender folks in the 2024 election campaign. And I know that the possibility of transgender women competing in amateur sports can present some questions of advantage— in a tiny number of cases across the country (according to the NCAA, 10 of 500,000 student athletes). I have no doubt that those challenges can be dealt with, on the basis of scientific and professional expertise, without the unravelling and malicious pressures of partisan politics. I also am certain that no progressive Tar Heel would throw some 80,000 North Carolina transgender citizens under the policymaking bus to appeal to the worst instincts of electoral politics. As one federal judge wrote recently, "In the self-truth that 'all people are created equal,' all means all— nothing more, nothing less." Rev. Pauli Murray put it this way, "There can be no compromise on the question of equality."

It is clear that North Carolinians cannot feel secure in their foundational liberties—liberties to, in Justice O'Connor's words, "define [their] own concept of existence, of meaning, of the universe, and the mystery of human life"—free of coercion by the state. Nor can they trust that Republican lawmakers won't (again) turn to ancient, but not dead, hatreds in order to cast some of our commonwealth's members as second- or third-class citizens or worse. Given that, not only is it essential to repeal North Carolina's antigay and antitransgender laws, I would welcome a one-sentence addition to Lieutenant Governor Hunt's Protect Women's Healthcare amendment (and its title), indicating, "Nor shall North Carolinians' fundamental right to privacy be denied."

Apparently, eleven states now include an expressed, textual guarantee of the right to privacy in their state constitutions. The US Constitution, it should be remembered, contains no such explicit privacy decree. State amendments, though not perfect, have offered judicial barriers to legislative efforts to force religious mandates on unconsenting, autonomous, independent persons of equal dignity. That sounds like a foundational Tar Heel notion to me.

Illustrating the urgency of rights to full membership, as this book went to the printer, the North Carolina General Assembly passed H.B. 850, hijacking an unrelated measure to offer "official recognition" that there are only two sexes in North Carolina. The statute also limited (nonexistent) state funding for transition procedures and made it more cumbersome to update sex designations on birth certificates. With the help of an unexplained and indefensible Democratic defection in the House, Governor Josh Stein's veto was overridden. Stein called the bill a "mean spirited attack on trans people." His veto message said: "My faith teaches that we are all children of God whatever our differences and that it is wrong to target vulnerable people as this legislation does." H.B. 850 reminds us that much of the work of constitutional liberty and equality in North Carolina lies ahead of us.

## CHAPTER SIX

★ ★ ★

# A Right to Economic Justice

## Fighting the Republican Commitment to Governing for Rich People

The central purpose of the North Carolina Republican Party is to make rich people richer and increase economic inequality in what is already the most economically unequal nation in the world. Some mission that is. I have opened, necessarily, with the methods that have been deployed by North Carolina Republicans to secure power, expand power, and eventually vest power in their hands permanently even at the cost of defeating democracy in the Tar Heel State. In this chapter, I turn to why they do all these things and why they commit these transgressions that are so definingly at odds with the American experiment. They do so to further line the already expansive pockets of wealthy people. In the process, they are delighted, additionally, if they can endow rich folks even more massively by taking away the all-too-meager resources of lower-income folks. Punishing the "unworthy" poor is apparently the icing on their political cake. North Carolina Republicans want to do much: They target Black Tar Heels; they rail and wage war against LGBTQ+ folks; they blame the shortcomings of the world, as they see them, on immigrants; they detest public schools and, especially, public school teachers; they whine, relentlessly, about all regulation, especially rules that protect the natural world from depredation; and they work endlessly to impose what they think of as their religion (which has decidedly nothing to do with the teachings of Jesus) on everyone else in the commonwealth. But the meta-goal of the North Carolina Republican Party, the ideal to which they return in every legislative session, year after year and decade after decade, is handing more resources to the rich and draining more of them from the poor. The main thing that is wrong with the United States, and North Carolina, in their singular and enduring view, is that poor people have too much and rich people don't have enough. It is the Republican need that can never be sated, the goal that is impossible to satisfy. There cannot be enough inequality to appease their defining urge. And far, far, far too often, Democrats let them get away with it.

I write that the United States is "the most economically unequal nation in the world." I don't mean to be flippant. Thomas Piketty, the French economist who has taught the world the most about economic polarization, wrote a few years ago that the United States embraces economic "inequality probably higher than in any other society, at any time in the past, anywhere in the world." Nobel Prize–winning economist Joseph Stiglitz echoed

Piketty, saying, "Since the mid-1970s the rules of the economic game have been re-written all over the world to advantage the rich and disadvantage the rest." The United States, Stiglitz noted, has "gone further in this perverse direction than in other developed countries." Author Kurt Andersen put it this way:

> From 1980 to 2015 in western Europe, the share of national income that went to the half of people below the median dipped from 24 to 22 percent—while in America the share going to the non-rich half has plummeted from 20 to 12 percent. Meanwhile the income share going to the richest western Europeans, the top 1 percent, has crept up from 10 to 12 percent—while in America it doubled to around 20 percent. In exceptional America, workers have been screwed and wealth inequality has become extreme.

And if the United States has become the world's great outlier in economic inequality, in the gap between rich and poor, North Carolina clearly visits greater hardship on those at the bottom than most US states do.

North Carolina Republican leaders claim endlessly that our economy is grand. It's not. Thirteen percent of Tar Heels, 1.3 million people, live in poverty, which is the seventeenth-highest rate among the fifty states. The poorest of Tar Heels, shamefully, are kids. Seventeen percent of children live in wrenching poverty—380,000 of them. This is the fifteenth-highest rate in the country. I've never heard a North Carolina Republican speak about child poverty. It's not part of their shtick. (It's just not cru-

cial to them, like the number of transgender kids on a middle-
school track team is.) A similar percentage of our children are
hungry, or, as it's put, food insecure. The number of North Carolinians living in poverty, or child poverty, or "deep" poverty
(defined as half the federal poverty rate of $29,000 for a family
of four), is also badly skewed by race. More than twice as many
Black, Latinx, and indigenous Tar Heels appear in those greatly
challenged categories compared to white Tar Heels. We have the
ninth-highest rate of poverty-level jobs, or jobs that pay so poorly
that working forty hours per week doesn't successfully lift one
out of poverty. A heavy majority of our low-wage workers are
women. Sixty percent of Tar Heels live paycheck to paycheck.
More than 1.5 million North Carolina workers, or 28 percent,
make less than seventeen dollars per hour, according to data from
Oxfam, a figure that is much higher than the national average (23
percent). North Carolina is not cordial to the bottom half. And
Republican leaders brag about that.

So, seeing such deprivation and inequality, what did North
Carolina Republicans do when they achieved full power in 2013?
The short answer is, by cruelly denying essential benefits to low-
income Tar Heels, instituting purposefully regressive taxation
programs that were designed to target and further burden low-
income adults and their children, and by directing massive tax
cuts toward North Carolina's wealthiest citizens and corporations, our General Assembly moved aggressively and enthusiastically to increase inequality and hardship. They did what they do
best: hand over huge sums to the already wealthy and take away

already far-too-thin resources from low-income folks. They displayed, in short, their unyielding commitment to rich people's government.

Immediately upon taking power, former Governor Pat McCrory, Senator Phil Berger, and then–NC House Speaker Thom Tillis rejected the Medicaid expansion that was offered by the federal government under the voluntary terms of the Patient Protection and Affordable Care Act. For more than a decade, that rejection meant that millions of Tar Heels were denied health care coverage, thousands died, tens of billions of federal health care dollars were turned away from the state, rural hospitals were closed, and hundreds of thousands of jobs were lost. No real explanation for the wounding decision was ever offered; it was simply repeated that expanding Medicaid wasn't "right" for North Carolina. Lawmakers seemed to declare that they just didn't believe in health care programs for low-income folks. If that meant that millions of impoverished North Carolinians would suffer, and thousands would even die, then too bad.

Next, the General Assembly, facing soaring unemployment rates, ushered in the largest cut to a state unemployment program in US history, moving North Carolina from the middle of the pack among state programs to the stingiest in the nation. When experts testified before the legislature that we had the most deficient unemployment scheme in the country, a key Republican lawmaker boasted, "I think where we are is a good thing."

In 2014, North Carolina became the first state in US history to abolish its earned income tax credit, thus raising the taxes of

working families that made about $35,000 per year. The Center
on Budget and Policy Priorities noted that North Carolina Republicans had earned the "dubious distinction" of being the only
US legislature to intentionally make it harder for low-income
working folks to support their children. This, too, seemed to
make lawmakers proud.

Large cuts to legal aid, food stamps, food banks, childcare
subsidies, school oral-health programs, and prekindergarten
classes ensued, even when, as with the Supplemental Nutrition
Assistance Program and the early stages of Medicaid expansion,
no savings to the state budget resulted whatsoever. Lawmakers
thought it essential that low-income Tar Heels understand that
Republicans wouldn't let even a willing federal government put
money in the pockets of impoverished North Carolinians. It was
the principle, after all.

And then came North Carolina's version of "tax reform."
Again in 2013, the General Assembly launched a multiyear effort
to ensure that low-income Tar Heels paid more in taxes while
wealthy folks paid much, much less. Lawmakers scrapped the
progressive income tax and replaced it with a flat tax, markedly
lowering the rate for the richest taxpayers. They did away with
the estate tax, which already applied only to estates worth more
than $5 million. A generous tax cut for corporations and addi-
tional shields for out-of-state business profits that were earned in
North Carolina followed. The General Assembly then increased
and extended regressive sales taxes, hitting up low-income folks
to help pay for new largesse aimed at the well heeled. They dou-

bled down on the project two years later, taxing an array of repair services, which fell even more squarely on low- and middle-
income payers. By 2016, the NC Budget & Tax Center found
that, with these adjustments, folks in the top 1 percent were getting a cut of $14,977 per year while those in the middle quin-
tile were receiving less than $100, and the bottom 40 percent of
taxpayers got tax increases instead of the advertised reductions.
Three-quarters of the total tax benefit went to the top 20 percent
of earners.

The pattern continues today. The General Assembly has put
in place legislation to reduce the personal income tax to 4.25
percent in 2025 and then to 2.49 percent in 2031. As boldly, the
corporate income tax rate will become 2 percent in 2025 and be
zeroed out entirely by 2030. And even before these (further) extreme changes attach, NC Budget & Tax Center and Institute on
Taxation and Economic Policy reports demonstrate that "more
than a decade of North Carolina tax cuts that have enriched the
wealthy, at the expense of the wellbeing of all," have left the state
and local tax system "upside down," with the poorest paying
most and the richest paying the least. Inequality "is made worse,
not improved," by North Carolina's tax policy. And that's saying
something.

In 2024, the shares of income paid, in state and local taxes, by
Tar Heels looked like this:

Lowest 20 percent of earners (less than $21,600): 10.5
    percent

Second lowest ($21,600–$42,200): 9.6 percent
Middle 20 percent ($42,200–$73,400): 9.3 percent
Fourth lowest ($73,400–$128,300): 9.1 percent
Next 15 percent ($128,300–$262,300): 8.5 percent
Next 4 percent ($262,300–$697,400): 7.2 percent
Top 1 percent (more than $697,400): 6 percent

Small wonder, I suppose, that the 2025 state senate budget aims to speed up the process and reduce the personal income tax rate to 1.99 percent by 2031. The servile work of catering to the rich and stepping on the necks of the poor, in North Carolina, is never done.

## Ending Rich People's Government

By now, I hope it is obvious that it is beyond crucial for North Carolina to end its regime of government for the wealthy and to adopt a taxation and regulatory structure that is designed to serve the interests of all, or as the North Carolina State Constitution puts it, "the good of the whole." Article I, Section 2 of our state charter declares the following: "All political power is vested in and derived from the people, all government of right originates from the people, is founded upon their will, and is instituted for the good of the whole."

It's not too much of a stretch, I'd suggest, to conclude that virtually the entire agenda of the North Carolina Republican General Assembly over the past fifteen years constitutes a rank and continuing violation of Article I, Section 2—its agenda of political suppression, its crusade to deny foundational personal constitutional rights, its outrageous trampling of the separation of powers, its intense politicization of judicial review, and, of course, its unyielding commitment to exalting the wealthy and crushing the poor. But even if that conclusion is not one to be brought before the courts, the North Carolina General Assembly must be commanded by the people of the state to focus its most dedicated attentions to the plight, interests, well-being, and future prospects of the everyday folks of North Carolina, especially low-income folks. The General Assembly must overtly recognize that average Tar Heels face an economic emergency. And it must act on that recognition.

No Democratic Party, or any progressive force whatsoever, can deem North Carolina's present economic framework acceptable. Few acts are more ethically reprehensible, and less democratically defensible, than deploying government power—persistently, pervasively, and usually dishonestly—to wound and further marginalize the most vulnerable in order to amass even larger fortunes for the powerfully privileged. But that is precisely what North Carolina Republicanism has delivered over the last fifteen years. In 2025, Democrats are required to repeat the stories of this cruelty every day and on every front. No one should be left confused about what has transpired. And Democrats must convince all Tar Heels that they will, in the months and years ahead, dismantle this entrenched landscape of government for the rich and replace it with a government for all.

I can say, perhaps most readily, how that might at least begin.
But I concede that others may have wiser suggestions or more
appealing remedies, both permanent and temporary. What I am
certain of, though, is that the North Carolina Democratic Party
has to become, and has to be seen as, the advocate for, the committed representative of, and the uncompromising voice for
working-class Tar Heels—the workaday folks who are so often
left out of our existing politics by both parties. I thought that a
protestor at 2024's May Day demonstrations in Raleigh, Nicole
Drapluk (aged 22), put it well: "It's more important now than
ever that we stand up, fight back, as a strong, united working
class." Votes should be taken every day, in the statehouse, to force
Republicans to reveal their defining fealty to the wealthy forces
that they serve. And Democrats should leave none confused that
they are the party seeking to pursue, day in and day out, "the
good of the whole."

Here are five steps to begin the process.

First, North Carolina Democrats should immediately begin to
return progressivity to the state tax structure. The current statutes that will reduce the income tax rate for individuals to 2.9
percent by 2029 and (as suggested by the state senate) to 1.99 percent in 2031 should be repealed. The same is true, perhaps even
more obviously, of the pending complete elimination of the corporate income tax. We certainly need no more tax changes that
are designed to meaningfully benefit only the wealthiest among
us. We've had our fill. Beyond that, higher levels of taxation for at
least the top one-third of North Carolina earners should be insti-

tuted, and parallel corporate tax rates should be restored. There is nothing fair or egalitarian about flat taxes in one of the most economically unequal societies on earth. And the idea that profitable corporations, including out-of-state ones, should be subsidized by the Tar Heels with the lowest incomes is, at the very least, nauseating. The days of special privileges for the rich in North Carolina should be at an end.

Second, North Carolina should rejoin the company of modern states and re-embrace an earned income tax credit. A dozen years ago, when the General Assembly acted to ensure that we became the only US state to repeal its earned income tax credit, NC Republicans demonstrated that they could be crueler to low-income people than any other legislature in the land. As a result, more than 900,000 Tar Heel low- and middle-income households received a significant state income tax increase. It's time to fix that outrage. With a resurrection of the earned income tax credit, North Carolina would join twenty-nine other states in easing the tax burden on working families who earn low wages: early childhood teachers, home health care workers, police officers, military services members, construction crews, and more. A new state earned income tax credit, pegged at 25 percent of the federal earned income tax credit, would benefit hundreds of thousands of Tar Heel families and, likely, more than a million children. The credit should be fully refundable, meaning that if a family owes less in taxes than the value of the credit, they still receive the full credit. It would be a crucial aid to family budgets in a time of stagnant wages, increased housing and childcare costs, and rising food prices. As important, it would help demonstrate to North Carolinians that their government is no longer at war with the state's lowest-income members and push back against a decade-long regime of regressive taxation. It should not be true that the Tar Heels with the least money pay the most in taxes. The implementation of a meaningful state earned income tax credit would cost less than the elimination of the corporate income tax. It would be, to understate, money immensely better spent.

Third, North Carolina should also follow the lead of fourteen other states and adopt a meaningful child tax credit. A humiliatingly high percentage of Tar Heel children live in poverty: almost one in five, which is one of the highest rates in the country. And we learned a lot about effective ways of dealing with child poverty during the COVID-19 crisis. Then, a temporarily expanded federal child tax credit reduced North Carolina's child poverty rate by an astonishing 42 percent (in 2021). Tragically, the US Congress allowed the federal credit to expire after the crisis, and the Republican North Carolina General Assembly failed to adopt a state substitute like many other state legislatures did. So, our child poverty rate once again soared to among the highest in the democratic world. That was, to be obvious, a North Carolina policy choice.

In 2025, North Carolina Democratic state senators Sophia Chitlik, Woodson Bradley, and Terence Everitt introduced a proposed child tax credit of $1,900 for each child aged six years old or younger as well as $1,600 for each child aged seven years old or older. The credit (which would also be refundable) would be directed toward low-income families, phasing out as salary levels rise. It would reduce child poverty in North Carolina by one-third. Studies across the country reveal that families that receive such a credit spend the savings on basics like childcare, housing, and school supplies, and the funds are linked to improved infant and maternal health and better educational performances and earning opportunities. As the Center on Budget and Policy Priorities has demonstrated, such credits are crucial "since large numbers of Americans work for low wages" and purchasing power is "substantially reduced among those concentrated in low wage occupations," especially when faced with otherwise-regressive taxation schemes. Earned income tax credits and child tax credits "promote work," increase "tax fairness," and "help families at virtually every stage of life." All North Carolina families with children have one thing in common: the intense desire to see those children thrive. Most would be decidedly annoyed to learn that North Carolina Republicans, through an array of taxation decisions, have made that more difficult than it is in many other states. Child poverty carries enormous costs in the Tar Heel State—costs in lost productivity, increased health care costs and crime, and child housing insecurity and abuse. It also makes us appear to be a heartless people. And we now know that it is possible to eradicate it.

Fourth, North Carolina must very significantly increase its minimum wage. We remain one of the twenty states that refuse to raise the minimum wage beyond the embarrassing, ancient, federal $7.25-per-hour standard. Our companions, of course, include the usual suspects: Alabama, Georgia, Kentucky, Louisiana, Mississippi, Oklahoma, South Carolina, Texas, and Tennessee (though Virginia's minimum wage is $12.41 per hour). North Carolina has not only continually refused to raise its standard, it has also taken various legal steps to prohibit any of its municipalities from acting to increase their own wage rules. Thirty states have higher wage standards than North Carolina, often even more than double what ours is. Ten states have minimum standards of fifteen dollars or more per hour, and scores of US municipalities enforce quite elevated minimum wage standards. The median, and the average, state standards are in the range of $11.00 or $11.50 per hour. North Carolina Republican lawmakers have, again, seemed proud that our wage requirement is the lowest in the country—or at least is notably tied for it. One assumes that if there were no mandatory federal floor, Tar Heel Republicans would demonstrate their profound regard for the plight of working North Carolinians by abolishing the minimum wage requirement altogether. Our bottom-of-the-barrel approach is one of the reasons why we have such high rates of poverty-level jobs. The great bulk of US states don't tolerate such wages. But we seem satisfied to cling to our feudal history. North Carolina progressives should demand the passage of a state constitutional amendment requiring the General Assembly to pass, each year, a minimum wage that is at least as high as the national average. We should reject outright Republicans' longstanding belief that North Carolina can only compete with other states economically by treating its workers worse than everyone else does. That's not a competition that we should seek to win.

Fifth, and finally, it is not possible to consider economic security, and economic fairness, in North Carolina without addressing health care as a fundamental human right. In December 2023, North Carolina, after more than a decade of resistance, became the fortieth state to expand eligibility for Medicaid. The federal-government-supported health insurance program was, as a result, opened to hundreds of thousands of low-income Tar Heels who were previously unable to afford insurance. More than 600,000 North Carolinians quickly achieved health care coverage. Expansion proved particularly beneficial in rural North Carolina.

The federal government presently pays 90 percent of the cost for expansion patients. A North Carolina "sign-on bonus" of $1.6 billion and an assessment on hospitals dramatically diminished the modest financial burdens on the state. Republican support for expansion was reportedly contingent on reduced state budgetary exposure. The statute-accepting expansion included a "trigger" provision that ends the agreement if the federal government ever fails to pay less than 90 percent of expansion costs.

The budget that was passed by the US House of Representatives in late February 2025 directed various congressional committees that oversee Medicaid to cut spending by almost $900 billion over the next decade—to offset President Donald Trump's trillions of dollars of tax breaks for the wealthiest of citizens. The deputy secretary of our state Medicaid program has indicated that North Carolina's expansion will be "discontinued" if the federal government reduces the 90 percent match. Hundreds of thousands of low-income Tar Heels would thus lose, completely, essential health care coverage, crushing their families, their prospects, their financial security, their health, and, in some cases, their lives.

North Carolinians have every reason not to trust the security of their health care to the Republicans of the General Assembly —though some Republican leaders, like State Rep. Donny Lambeth of Winston-Salem, have acted heroically to expand Medicaid. And the US health care system is a radically complex admixture of federal, state, and private initiatives. So, identifying a precise individual remedy for North Carolina's low-income health care challenges is likely impossible. But what must be clear is that progressives will not tolerate moving backward on access to health care in the Tar Heel State. North Carolina must finish the work of ensuring universal health care coverage. And, to be obvious, that foundational goal is more important than offering a new suite of tax reductions for the richest of our citizens and their out-of-state corporate friends.

For me, these are five places where a North Carolina crusade for economic justice can begin. Others may have more compelling ideas. And, as ever, once progress is achieved in one arena, others will readily suggest themselves. What is crucial, however, is that North Carolina Democrats press the cause of low- and-middle-income Tar Heels as *the* defining mission of the party. In the process, of course, Republicans will continually demonstrate their unyielding opposition to economic efforts to bolster the plight of the bottom half. They will then, perhaps, lose their North Carolina superpower—lying, pretending to be committed to ordinary Tar Heels while actually serving only the interests of the wealthiest among us, talking the regular folks' game while acting, always, as handservants to the rich.

## CHAPTER SEVEN

★ ★ ★

# A Right to the Best Possible Public Education

Today, education is perhaps the most important function of
state and local governments. It is required in the performance of our
most basic public responsibilities. It is the very foundation of good
citizenship. It is doubtful any child may reasonably be expected to
succeed in life if denied the opportunity of (effective) education.
Such an opportunity, when the state has undertaken to provide it,
is a right to be made available to all on equal terms.
—*Brown v. Board of Education of Topeka,* 1954

N orth Carolinians are deeply committed to public
education. It is in the blood, in Tar Heel DNA. It has
been so for countless generations. It is, particularly in
the South, seen as the central pathway out of poverty.
It is the cornerstone of our belief in generational progress and
the core notion that our kids will have better prospects than we
had. It is a principal tool of civic engagement and cultural inter-
dependence; it is democracy's workhorse. It is born of our foundational belief in universal human dignity. And it is the framework for our embrace of community, both public and private. It

is, unsurprisingly, etched into the pages of the North Carolina
State Constitution.

Article I, Section 15 of the state constitution's declaration of
rights ordains that "the people have a right to the privilege of education, and it is the duty of the State to guard and maintain that
right." As the North Carolina Supreme Court has long noted, it is
not a mere suggestion, it is compulsory. It sets forth an affirmative
duty for North Carolina's government to "guard and maintain" the
people's right to education. And the responsibility is "not merely
administrative, but financial," lying ultimately "on the shoulders of
one entity, the State." Article IX, Section 2(1) provides that "the
General Assembly shall provide by taxation and otherwise for a
general and uniform system of free public schools, wherein equal
opportunities shall be provided for all students."

The text and placement of these provisions are telling. Our
high court has explained:

> The plain text of these provisions emphasizes the distinctive
> prominence of public education within our Constitution:
> it is first established as a positive right of the people within
> the Declaration of Rights, then mandated to be guarded
> and maintained by the State, then specifically required to
> be funded through taxation and otherwise by the General
> Assembly.

Constitutional provisions, I can attest, are often vague and
standardless. Here, for once, the directions are designed to be
clear, prescriptive.

Perhaps because of the duty-based precision of these state constitutional mandates, North Carolina has seen more litigation
and has provoked and produced more systemic study of the challenges and shortcomings of its "general and uniform system of
public schools . . . wherein equal opportunities [are] provided for
all students" than most state governments. It is fair to say that, by
2025, we well know what we have.

In July 1997, the North Carolina Supreme Court decided, in
*Leandro v. State*, that the NC State Constitution establishes a
right to substantively adequate educational opportunities, not
merely opened schoolhouse doors. Republican and Democratic
justices agreed unanimously:

> The right to education provided in the state Constitution is
> a right to a sound basic education. An education that does
> not serve the purpose of preparing students to participate
> and compete in the society in which they live and work is
> devoid of substance and is constitutionally inadequate.

Subsequent state supreme court rulings in 2004 and 2022,
and trial court determinations attempting to enforce *Leandro*'s
decision for the last twenty-five years, have doubled down on the
constitutional promise.

Judge Howard Manning repeatedly found that "the poor academic performance of at-risk students is too widespread to by-
pass and put off for another day." Clear and convincing evidence,
he wrote, demonstrated that "at-risk children throughout North
Carolina are not obtaining a sound basic education." Accord-

ingly, "the State of North Carolina is ORDERED to remedy the constitutional deficiency for those children who are not being provided the basic educational services" demanded by the state constitution. By 2016, Judge David Lee (Judge Manning's successor) found "the court record is replete with evidence that the *Leandro* right continues to be denied to hundreds of thousands of North Carolina schoolchildren." In 2019, the massive, scholarly, court-ordered WestEd report, which documented the North Carolina public school system's failure of constitutional compliance, concluded that "the state is further away from meeting its constitutional obligation to provide every child with the opportunity for a sound basic education than it was when the Supreme Court announced the *Leandro* decision more than 20 years ago."

Most pointedly, the WestEd study, which was ordered and accepted by the various tribunals, found the following:

> More than 400,000 students—over a quarter of the students in North Carolina—attend 843 high poverty schools in the state—representing a third of students statewide. Equal opportunity for a sound basic education is compromised in these high poverty schools. They have fewer teachers who are fully licensed, who have advanced degrees, and who have achieved National Board of Professional Teaching Standards Certification. They have more lateral-entry teachers and early career teachers who have been shown to be less effective. Students in high poverty schools experience cumulative disadvantages that constrain their oppor-

tunity to learn. The outcomes set forth in the *Leandro* rulings are not being met.

As Judge Lee concluded, "North Carolina's Pre-K public education system leaves too many students behind, especially students of color and economically disadvantaged students.... As a result, thousands of students are not being prepared for full participation in the global, interconnected economy and the society in which they will live, work, and engage as citizens."

Unsurprisingly perhaps, national studies conducted in 2024 indicated that average teacher pay in North Carolina is forty-third in the nation and per-pupil spending is a humiliating forty-eighth in the nation. Tar Heel teachers make, on average, almost $14,000 less than the national average of $72,030. Alabama pays its teachers decidedly more ($3,600) than North Carolina does. Only the good folks of Kansas, Mississippi, Florida, West Virginia, Louisiana, Montana, South Dakota, and Missouri pay less. North Carolina ranks behind all its neighboring states: Georgia (twenty-third), Virginia (twenty-sixth), South Carolina (thirty-sixth), and Tennessee (thirty-eighth).

In the summer and fall of 2021, Judge Lee issued orders requiring the North Carolina General Assembly to report its progress in ensuring funding for a massive *Leandro* remedial plan. The legislature failed to do so. Lee then ordered the transfer of hundreds of millions of dollars in state funds to support a multiyear effort. Republican leaders challenged the orders, sending the case, for the fourth time, to the state supreme court in November 2022.

The justices determined, yet again, that "as in 2004, far too many North Carolina schoolchildren, especially those marginalized, are not afforded their constitutional right to the opportunity of a sound basic education." For "twenty-five years," the justices concluded, "the judiciary has deferred to the executive and legislative branches to implement a comprehensive solution to this ongoing violation; today that deference expires."

Republican leaders again challenged aspects of the decision (noting, no doubt, the changed political makeup and altered behavior of the NC Supreme Court). Though oral arguments took place in February 2024, no new ruling has been issued. Surely, one is forthcoming. The court seems interested in the political timing of its intervention, like backroom bosses. No doubt the overtly partisan tribunal will weaken or completely displace the *Leandro* mandate, casting twenty-five years of precedent, promise, and struggle into the trash bin. It will likely do so through some jurisdictional, or remedial, or "political question"–based procedural determination. One thing it won't be able to do is deny the accuracy of more than two decades' worth of determinations that the state of North Carolina, each day, fails to provide a "uniform system of free public schools wherein equal opportunities [are] provided for all students."

## Vouchers

If North Carolina's legislative leaders have struggled stubbornly, implacably, and ingeniously for decades to escape their constitutionally imposed obligation to create and support a public school system that sustains and provides equal prospects to low-income and marginalized students; it is important to understand that our Republican leaders are not always stingy about education. When it comes to utterly standardless, unaccredited, and educationally unaccountable private schools, which discriminate potently on the basis of race, religion, sexuality, income, disability, geography, "morality," and "biblical lifestyle" (for example, requiring "born again" status, being dedicated to "Jesus Christ as Lord," or specifically rejecting "Mormons, Muslims, Jehovah's Witnesses, and Non-Messianic Jews"), our Republican General Assembly has revealed a generosity undiscovered in other arenas. They may detest public schools, but these bastions of separation, inequality, polarization, and traditional privilege are just their huckleberry. Private, voucher-driven, religious schools, which provide new ways to avoid the foundational charge of *Brown v. Board of Education* and further drain resources from economically distressed rural North Carolina to lavish dollars on more generously funded urban schools, are the favored offspring of the North Carolina Republican Party. They may have no sworn constitutional obligation to support them. In fact, such schools are often themselves both constitutionally problematic and educationally unsound. But Republican lawmakers regularly encourage them to seek, and spend, even more. Not all schools are pariahs, just public ones.

North Carolina's massive voucher program, ironically called "Opportunity Scholarship," was launched in 2014. Initially, scholarship eligibility was based on a family's income, and the money was used to pay tuition for eligible students at private K–12 schools. At the outset, the "school choice" program was modest (1,200 participants) and directed only at low-income families. In 2023, the General Assembly expanded the scheme, as had long been predicted, to allow scholarships to be given to all families regardless of income and to students who had already been attending private schools on their own. House Bill 10, which then-Governor Roy Cooper attempted to veto, now provides state funding for students who attend private schools, no matter how wealthy their families are. Massive funding increases also have followed. In 2025, voucher funding was raised to an amazing $594 million. It is projected that billions more will be allocated to the fund over the next decade. Currently, applicants are divided into four income tiers. In 2024, 79,775 students received vouchers. Forty-two percent of the successful recipients came from the two highest income tiers, meaning each family made more than $115,000 per year. Fourteen percent came from families that made more than $250,000 per year. Only 30 percent of recipients came from families that earned $57,000 or less per year. A disproportionate 74 percent were white. In the summer of 2024, the State Board of Education reported that only 6,710 of the 80,325 new Opportunity Scholarship recipients attended public schools the preceding year. The great majority of new vouchers went to subsidize students who were already in private institutions. While the Republican General Assembly gave the back of the hand to students from low-income families and its constitutionally imposed obligations to the public schools under

*Leandro*, it offered massive subsidies to students from the richest families under the Opportunity Scholarship scheme.

And there's more.

A November 2024 study by ProPublica examined the use of state vouchers to support North Carolina "segregation academies," or schools that were established across the South for white children during the desegregation era (1960s and 1970s). They determined that thirty-nine such institutions are still in operation and now receiving voucher funds. Twenty of the schools reported student bodies that were at least 85 percent white. The schools brought in more than $20 million between 2021 and 2024. None reflected the "demographics of their communities." Northeast Academy, a small Christian school in Northampton County, is 99 percent white in a county that is only 40 percent white. It received $438,500 from the voucher program in 2022, which was almost half its tuition income. Lawrence Academy, established in Bertie County in 1968, "has never had a Black enrollment higher than 3% in a county whose population hovers around 60% Black." A small school with fewer than 300 students, it received $518,240 in vouchers in 2023. Otis Smallwood, superintendent of the cash-strapped public schools in Bertie County, told ProPublica that he "tries not to be political," but "that's a half-million dollars that could be put to better benefit in the public schools." The ProPublica study concluded, more broadly, "Opportunity Scholarships don't always live up to their name for Black children." Private schools don't have to take everyone, and they don't have to provide transportation or free meals. Black parents are "less likely to be able to afford the difference between a voucher of $7,468 a year and an annual tuition bill that can top $10,000 or even $20,000."

Finally, as Public Schools First NC has shown, the dramatically expanded voucher-program increases are "highly concentrated in urban and suburban areas, further straining resources for rural areas that already struggle to fund their public schools." Twenty-two of North Carolina's 100 counties have no private schools. But private schools in more-affluent Wake County received $13.9 million in 2023–2024 and more than $56.1 million in 2025, amounting to a one-year increase of $42.5 million. Since the Opportunity Scholarship program was initiated in 2014, Wake County private schools have received $105,794,785; Cumberland County schools have been awarded $99,826,737; Mecklenburg County has obtained $83,254,416; Guilford County has received $70,508,431; and Forsyth County has been granted $43,165,849. The five counties together have amassed almost $400 million. And this is, to understate, rising.

The *Leandro* requirement of a sound basic education for every Tar Heel kid is often most powerfully challenged, and notably unmet, in the impoverished rural communities of North Carolina. Our Republican General Assembly has also stubbornly refused to meet its constitutionally prescribed obligations to students from low-income families, particularly in rural North Carolina. The Opportunity Scholarship voucher scheme, ironically, further siphons resources from our poorest places and redirects them to wealthier ones. Sadly, that can no longer come as a surprise.

And the outrage is made worse by a program that bolsters our tragic history of racial segregation, abandons all pretense of educational accountability and rigor, purposely crushes the wall of separation between church and state, and forces some Tar Heels to subsidize schools that teach that they are abominations.

## Requiring a Sound, Basic Public Education for All

Achieving a "sound, basic public education" for all children can seem, after nearly three decades of frustration and retrenchment, like an almost unattainable goal for North Carolinians. It is not, of course, as our history of progress and combat shows. But, in a larger sense, the goal is a modest one. It seeks to ensure the basics, the necessities, the undeniable. It does not demand what a confident and optimistic constitutional democracy would seek to ensure: the best possible education for every child in North Carolina regardless of zip code, background, race, or economic status. None are to be deemed unworthy. None are forgotten. All children, every single one, should receive the best we can possibly provide. And we should do for each kid everything that we would try to do for our own. Surely that is what our true beacon should be.

But a "sound, basic public education" is a workable legal norm. Doing the best job possible is probably not. And it is the vineyard in which we have toiled, year in and year out, for more than a generation. Heroes have labored, teaching us, leading us, and carrying forward North Carolina's banner of educational equity.

It should remain our lodestar regardless of what a lawless and
purposely inegalitarian North Carolina Supreme Court, in the
months and years ahead, shall decree. So, Democrats and progressives should push to fully fund *Leandro*'s dictates, carrying
out the case's foundational plans, as future generations of the NC
General Assembly update its aspirations and demands. It is also
certain that North Carolia's Opportunity Scholarship plan—its
private voucher program—is directly and purposefully at odds
with *Leandro*'s requirement of a sound, basic public education
for every North Carolina child. Our vouchers are meant to displace Article IX's required "general and uniform system of free
public schools," not to fulfill it. But the Republicans of the North
Carolina General Assembly are not empowered to eliminate the
constitutional rights and responsibilities of Article I, Section 9
and Article IX even if they detest them. They would be required
to amend the state constitution to ditch North Carolina's defining commitment to an equal public education for every child.
And that they could never do.

North Carolina's primary tool of egalitarian democratic implementation—free, equal, effective public education—should not
be dependent on the vagaries and, often, greedy and exclusionary
instincts of lawmakers of either political party. North Carolina's
children would benefit immensely, both now and in generations
to come, from a state constitutional amendment along the following lines:

North Carolina has long required that the General Assembly provide for, by taxation, a general and uniform system

of public schools wherein equal opportunities are afforded to all students. Every child in North Carolina therefore enjoys the right to a sound, basic, public education provided for and maintained by the State. The State's public education obligation is mandatory, by duty, not suggestion. It is enforceable through the North Carolina courts. State-based payments for private or religious schools are inconsistent with the requirements of a general and uniform system of public schools and are therefore prohibited.

## CHAPTER EIGHT

# The Commands of Climate Change

## GENE NICHOL & PATRICK BRADEY

I n September 2019, Hurricane Dorian brought a powerful storm surge ashore in North Carolina, swallowing the whole community of Cedar Island. Cedar Island is nearer to the mainland than North Carolina's Outer Banks barrier islands, and so is home to none of the herds of wild Banker horses, which are descendants of strays that have called the islands home since the first Europeans landed there four centuries ago. But Cedar Island's residents do count among their number some unusual neighbors: a small herd of feral cattle, no more than a few dozen in all. Dorian's waters swept these cows out to sea, adrift in a calamity beyond their understanding. Some were later found on nearby islands, where, by certain estimates, they had arrived through a perilous journey of nearly forty miles as they were tossed back and forth upon the waves for hours. Those that survived their trial at sea were eventually returned to Cedar Island. Two months later, one of those cows gave birth; the calf, as

J. B. MacKinnon put it, had been "baptized" in the waters of the tempest.

Since our earliest history, North Carolinians have been braving the volatile wilds of the state's climate. In 1693, a hurricane rocked the eastern shore with such violence that "it seemed to reverse the order of nature," rerouting rivers and recarving the inlets of the coastline. The struggles against the forces of nature that shaped our state have continued unabated. And in recent decades, an exacerbation of the struggle has notably accelerated our challenges: the mounting crisis that threatens the water, skies, soil, homes, businesses, farmland, forests, and built infrastructures that we rely on for daily life.

I'm no climate expert—by a good stretch. I'm a seventy-four-year-old constitutional lawyer. Still, this is a book about a progressive political agenda for North Carolina. And it doesn't take much expertise to recognize that no discussion of public policy challenges in the Tar Heel State—or anywhere in the country, or the globe, for that matter—can be candid, relevant, or complete without attention to the burgeoning threat that is the climate crisis. It is the issue that is positioned to subsume all others, the peril that encompasses everything, today and in the months and years to come. My goal here is perhaps no more ambitious than to identify the climate's centrality, noting some of North Carolina's particulars, and adding a note (that is made far more compellingly by others) of its urgency. I am happy and relieved to be joined in writing this chapter by a young colleague, one who is better schooled and better versed: Patrick Bradey. The work here, I shall simply say, is much enhanced by his efforts. No one can afford the luxury of ignoring the climate in North Carolina even if it is outside one's wheelhouse.

Since 2010, the climate crisis here has seemingly gained in velocity and reach. Hurricane Matthew (in 2016) and Hurricane Florence (in 2018) ravaged the eastern half of the state, in some cases submerging major roadways to create a new kind of inland island that isolated large swaths of the Coastal Plain, trapping people in their towns for days on end as they waited for relief to arrive. They represent symptoms of a growing tide of increasingly frequent, increasingly dangerous, and increasingly damaging storms that plague the Southeast as the Atlantic hurricane season gets longer and more extreme, propelled by warming waters and volatile ocean winds. In July 2025, Tropical Storm Chantal caused record flooding throughout the upper Piedmont including Chapel Hill, and in some places, waters crested above the historic highs of Hurricane Fran thirty years ago. Nearly a hundred people required rescue from the rising waters, and at least six people lost their lives as creeks and rivers rose faster than the water could be outrun.

Even places that were once thought to be immune from the impacts of climate change are being forced to reckon with the cataclysmic power of these weather events. Tropical Storm Fred brought devastating flooding to the mountain valleys of western North Carolina in 2021—a harbinger of an even worse disaster that was only a few years ahead. Three years later, Hurricane Helene dumped biblical amounts of water across a huge

swath of Appalachia, inundating rivers and lakes to levels never
before documented in the recorded history of the region. The
city of Asheville, which sits nestled in the Blue Ridge Mountains,
more than 2,000 feet above sea level, was cut off from the world
as floodwaters washed away roads and bridges that led into town,
and the municipal water system was damaged so severely that it
could not be repaired for weeks. Smaller towns were even less for-
tunate; some were nearly wiped off the map. With more than 100
fatalities and nearly $60 billion in damages in North Carolina
alone, Helene was the most fatal storm the state had experienced
in more than 150 years, and it was its most expensive ever. And
this from a storm focused along a band of earth more than 250
miles away from the Atlantic Ocean.

The increased devastation of waters invading inward from the
sea and falling downward from the opened skies carries a layered
impact beyond the immediate damage that is surveyed by tele-
vision cameras. A rising sea level means greater seepage of water into the earth farther and farther inland, eating away at the
foundations of homes and floating caskets long at rest up to the
surface. The salt of this water slowly eats away at buried pipes,
destroying by a thousand cuts the water mains and other critical
infrastructures that hold our communities together, causing hundreds of thousands of dollars in damage every year. At the same
time, that salinity drains the life from the soil of the Coastal Plain.
The long agricultural heritage that loamy earth has supported for
generations is gradually dying as the soil health is degraded to a

point at which it can no longer support the same bounty that
made the east such a characteristic and unique community.

And it is not water alone that marches onward as a threat to
us and our neighbors. In a perverse parallel, wildfires are similarly becoming more common, both in the western mountains
and the eastern pine forests. Dryer seasons allow fuels to accumulate, which are exploited by more-frequent wind events to
carry any ignition farther and faster than they would be able to
travel otherwise. The droughts that exacerbate these fires similarly threaten agricultural viability, restrict recreational activities,
hasten the erosion of vulnerable soils, and facilitate even more
rapid saltwater intrusion.

Our General Assembly has often assumed a posture of willful
ignorance with respect to the changing climate. When, in 2010,
the state's scientific and coastal management agencies predicted
that sea levels could rise by more than three feet by the end of
the century, presenting an imminent and existential risk to more
than 2,000 square miles of North Carolina and the families that
call it home, the legislature took swift action, passing a law that
commanded that the state would no longer be allowed to predict
an accurate rate of sea-level rise, instead being limited to the out-
dated figures which the state's Republican leadership would pre-
scribe for them. They did so at the urging of local governments
and real-estate development firms that were upset about what re-
alistic scientific predictions would do to their profit margins.

Stephen Colbert was merciless on *The Late Show*:

If your science gives you a result you don't like, pass a law saying the result is illegal. Problem solved. Bravo North Carolina. By making this bold action on climate change today, you're ensuring that when it actually comes, you'll have plenty of options, or at least two: sink or swim.

But, of course, Republican lawmakers could perhaps be expected to obscure the true nature of the climate problems that we now face since they are, in no small part, of their own design. In 2021, the state seemed to make some progress, passing a law requiring major utilities to more than halve their carbon emissions by the end of the decade with the goal of carbon neutrality by 2050. That first deadline was nixed, however, by legislation that passed the state senate in 2025, citing the urgency of the climate crisis as "arbitrary" and responding to the need of big businesses to meet "growing demand." Governor Stein's eventual veto could not be successfully sustained. The regression was particularly galling at a moment when climate experts assert that emissions must be decreasing if we are to preserve a livable planet; every moment we delay makes the problem bigger and the solution harder to implement.

The quick backstep was par for the course. Lawmakers have made it harder for local governments to fund their own public transit systems and placed a high priority on the development of new roads and highways without concern for those systems' contributions to emissions that exacerbate climate change. And the continued emphasis on carbon-belching projects, including possible delays of coal-fired–power plant retirement dates and the proposed development of a fleet of new gas-fired power plants, draws attention away from the sustainable developments and clean-energy projects that could be the state's focus.

These warnings aren't just the forebodings of academics yelling, "The sky is falling!" Even major insurance companies are waking up to the risk that climate change poses in North Carolina, joining the chorus raising the alarm about the threat that it poses to the state's future. Their own projections show that home values in vulnerable areas will fall as climate change progresses. They intend to raise insurance rates to cover the increased risk; statewide premiums have risen nearly 30 percent over the last four years and are slated to jump another 30 percent in many coastal areas as long as the General Assembly leaves us sitting square in the crosshairs of the next major disaster.

The effort that is required of us is nearly Herculean. It will demand economic, political, and social mobilization at a scale unlike any other challenge we've yet been made to meet. But its form is familiar, the science and the tools are known to us, and the stakes are now beyond clear.

## A Light on the Shoreline

The lighthouse at Cape Hatteras has stood as a beacon to sailors along North Carolina's shores since 1870, watching over a segment of the coast that is so infamously perilous it has earned the moniker Graveyard of the Atlantic. Built to withstand the wind and waves and guide the tempest-tost to the light of day, the lighthouse required its own rescue to meet the sea's threat. By 1999, the earth on which the lighthouse stood had gradually been eaten away over the past century, and without action, the lighthouse itself would soon have been consumed by the waves. In a stunning feat of engineering, the lighthouse was lifted from its foundations and shifted more than a half-mile farther inland. Today, the Cape Hatteras Lighthouse stands as a reminder that Tar Heels can rise to meet and overcome seemingly insurmountable challenges, including climate change.

In the most general sense, climate policy falls into two main buckets: mitigation and adaptation. Mitigation looks forward, focusing on ways to stop the progression of the climate crisis and addressing the types and volumes of emissions we spill into the air and that contribute to the volatility of the earth's delicate systems. Adaptation is concerned with the present and finding ways to protect ourselves from the bought-and-paid-for impacts that we know we will have to face. Neither alone is enough to carry us through the storm, but together, they light the way to preserve the North Carolina that we know and love.

## Stopping the Storm

Mitigation efforts cover a broad spectrum of work, but they are all calculated to lower the amount of greenhouse gas emissions that human activity throws into the air. North Carolina's since-altered plan to compel Duke Energy to lower its emissions by set amounts along a publicly mandated timeline was one such measure, aiming to hold our state's goliath to account for its climate damage. A lot of mitigation efforts focus on the sources of carbon emissions, principally electric power generation and transportation, which together account for more than half of national carbon emissions. But mitigation work can take different forms, from expanding the ways that we produce our power by promoting wind and solar development to encouraging urban-planning policies and public transit development that reduce our reliance on cars and revamping efficiency standards for new construction and other industries that reduce the strain on our existing systems.

The fact is that emissions are a global problem, contributed to by billions of sources across the entire world, and North Carolina alone will not turn back the clock on carbon and fix climate change. But greenhouse gas emissions accumulate in the atmosphere, contributing to destabilizing climate warming for decades after fossil fuels are burned. Because the emissions are cumulative, the need is pressing to ratchet them down sooner rather than later by shifting our economy to clean, renewable energy resources as rapidly as possible. That transition also brings a myriad of benefits that are not always accounted for by the NC Utilities Commission or the Department of Transportation. David Neal, of the Southern Environmental Law Center, explained that experts have shown that if we count the health benefits that would result from shutting down dirty coal power plants, gas-fired electric power plants and boilers, and transitioning away from transportation with tailpipe emissions, those benefits alone would more than pay for the energy transition. We in North Carolina have an obligation to our people—those who live here today and those who will live here tomorrow—to do our part in the generational undertaking that this work represents. And we already have tools to do it.

North Carolina has some of the most prime real estate in the country for the expansion of wind-generated energy—about twenty-five miles off the coast. In 2021, then-Governor Roy Cooper directed state agencies to develop plans that would enable our state to develop enough wind-energy infrastructure to equal almost one-third of North Carolina's power needs by 2040. Though offshore wind development is subject to a morass of federal permitting strictures, states are empowered with significant discretion in the planning of their offshore areas, and a more muscular state-level climate administrative apparatus could assume a greater degree of the scientific and technical review work that is necessary to carry these projects over the finish line (especially as experts are increasingly exiled from the federal workforce). North Carolina also has onshore wind potential, which even Duke Energy has included as part of its "least cost" path for meeting state electricity demands. Looking more broadly, Governor Josh Stein has noted that North Carolina is "at a crossroads." "Climate change makes events like Helene more likely." We are charged with making North Carolina "safer, stronger, cleaner, and more resilient," he reported, and can have "economic success as we pursue a cleaner, more cost-effective energy future."

Even at the local level, we can expect our leaders to do more to chip away at the mosaic of efforts that will be required to meet this moment. Many cities across the state are already taking steps to electrify their vehicle fleets; Charlotte even purchased an all-electric fire truck, which was the first to enter service anywhere in the Southeast. Others are introducing new zoning policies that make it easier to build more housing units closer to the places where people work, shop, and recreate, thus reducing our need to drive as often or as far within our own communities. Localities are expanding their mass-transit options and connecting transit to bicycle and pedestrian greenways, providing options for reduced reliance on single-occupancy motor vehicles. Still others are actively developing and protecting parks and green spaces that act as localized carbon sinks, pulling emissions out of the air and helping to moderate urban temperatures.

We can engage with private partners to accelerate a cleaner transition, rolling out more efficient consumer products to market that reduce the demand for carbon emissions and lower monthly electric bills despite the General Assembly's efforts to cut electric-innovation tax credits that threaten thousands of jobs and billions of dollars in business investment in North Carolina. Growing the economy and protecting the climate aren't in a zero-sum competition. The Research Triangle anchors some of the leading technology firms on earth and is a hub for innovations in battery technologies that will be essential to a climate-smart future.

## Riding the Waves

While mitigation looks forward at how we can reduce our con-tinuing contribution to the climate crisis, adaptation considers what we are going to do about the very immediate or certainly imminent impacts of a changing climate. Mitigation seeks to keep the problem from getting worse, and adaptation deals with the problems that we already have. As the people of Asheville can attest, that problem requires urgent attention.

Interstate 40, which collapsed into the Pigeon River as it snaked through the mountains as a result of Hurricane Helene in the fall of 2024, and North Carolina Highway 12, which follows the spine of the Outer Banks and is frequently blocked by storm debris and shifting sands, both illustrate the vulnerabilities of our transportation infrastructure to climate hazards. And rural wa-ter systems across eastern North Carolina are increasingly prone to degradation by saltwater intrusion into aging pipes that leach away at their strength and at the lifeblood of small-town living that has been so central to our state's identity. Hardening both to the increasing impacts of water and rain will be a vital part of our defenses against climate risks.

But the natural environment is not only the line of attack along which these risks march forward on our homes and neigh-bors, it can also be our best defense. Nurturing wetlands and es-tuaries lets them continue their ancient function of absorbing storm surges and buffering the worst of the waves that pummel the shores. And agricultural operations can adopt small-scale but widespread practices that conserve soil use, help sequester carbon in the ground, protect from unnecessary erosion, and diversify crop types and livestock breeds to those that are more resilient to hotter, drier conditions.

Even at the household level, small changes can make an impact on our ability to weather the storm together. In hurricane-prone areas, where the state has already been called on to serve as the insurer of last resort because major insurance companies have made it nearly impossible to secure coverage for homes and businesses, a family can get a rebate on their premium for installing a "super-roof" that is less likely to blow off in major storms and is hardened against leakage from intense rains. The program pays for itself through fewer storm losses and is a model for the micro-scale adaptations that add together to make a meaningful difference to our quality of life in a new climate reality.

## A Promise to Our Children

The North Carolina State Constitution provides helpfully, "It shall be the policy of this State to conserve and protect its lands and waters for the benefit of all its citizenry." It also commands that the state pursue "every other appropriate way to preserve as a part of the common heritage of this State its forests, wetlands, estuaries, beaches, historical sites, open lands, and places of beauty." The section explicitly calls for our governments, both state and local, "to control and limit the pollution of our air and water."

But our courts' treatment of that language has been mixed. It has generally been understood to grant governments the legal ability to regulate the use of, damage to, and disposition of the state's land, air, and water or to bring suits as trustees of those resources on our behalf. But it has never been held to include an enforceable right that can be asserted by an individual and raised in defense of a community. Despite any creative arguments that could be mustered to suggest that the state constitution's language, as written, encompasses an actionable right to a sustainable future, our courts seem disinclined to agree. And any more congenial interpretation now has to overcome the barriers of precedent and tradition.

Therefore, we press for constitutional language making the case of crisis and obligation:

> The people of North Carolina, individually and as a whole, now and into perpetuity, are entitled to the right of a clean and healthful environment, which includes a livable climate, and it shall be the duty of this State to conserve and protect its air, lands, and waters for the benefit of the people of the state, nation, and the world. The State and its subdivisions shall have power to acquire, regulate, develop, and preserve the air, lands, and waters of this State and to foster a transition away from fossil fuels.

This change could prove important in several ways. First, it makes clear that the right to a sustainable future belongs to both the individual and the community and extends, explicitly, to the commands of the climate. The community framing makes clear the nature of the issues that are under threat and the personal attachments that transform shared interests into ones that are enforceable by law. Rather than it being the *policy* of the state to engage in climate work, it would become the *duty* of the state. And rather than owing this duty to the people of North Carolina alone, the obligation is to the world at large, recognizing the unique natural heritage of this place and the global scale of the challenges we face and share.

Our own storm is coming; it is upon us now. We will be, and we are now, caught up in its tempest. Whether we will be drawn under or emerge as a changed, and stronger, North Carolina remains, as always, in our hands.

## CHAPTER NINE

★ ★ ★

# The Obligation of Engaged Citizens
## Defending Democracy by Doing Democracy

When former President Lyndon Johnson signed the famed Civil Rights Act of 1964, he told the nation the following: "My fellow citizens, we live in a time of testing. We must not fail. I urge every American to join in this effort to bring justice and hope to all our people."

A time of testing—that it was. As is it now.

And what a surprise it is to many of us, in 2025—in Washington, DC, and in Raleigh—how thorough, how complete, and how unyielding our testing is. Who would have thought that a US president would exercise dictatorial powers, gathering all authority unto himself, and wield those never-before-seen prerogatives in cruelty to intimidate and terrify as he attempts to clear the continent (and beyond) of opposition? Who would have thought that at the same time, in North Carolina, one political party would illegitimately amass, and vest, such disproportionate political and judicial power that constitutional democracy could be effectively thwarted so that lawmakers could boldly rule without the consent of the governed? Who would have thought that judges would become so habituated to lawlessness that traditions of judicial review and accountability would be sundered and the historic commands of *Marbury v. Madison* would be mocked, defiled, and then simply set aside as if a government of laws was primitive, obsolete, and naïve?

And Tar Heels, over generations, have been through so much, suffered and sacrificed so much, and made so much headway that they came to be regarded as potential beacons of progress across the South. Who would have anticipated that old doors of racial and political suppression would have been enthusiastically reopened as if a hard-won history could be beneficially cast aside and prerogatives of tribe could overcome the demands of equality and freedom, creating tiers of citizenship and privileges of race and religion, and ushering in new frontiers of dominance that are inimical to the promise of the United States? Who would have thought that this is the road that we would come to travel, as if our past meant nothing and our much-pledged aspirations were mere mantras to hypocrisy?

Many North Carolinians are surprised by our threatened and now developing fate. I am. But in a deeper sense, our surprise is unmerited. It is born of ignorance and a lack of curiosity, rooted in a willingness to assume that prior chapters of our history were less brutal, and less continuous, than they are. Black North Carolinians are more apt to be surprised at white folks' surprise at

our resumed antidemocratic crusade and to find our assumptions
of progress propagandistic. I remember, for example, when I was
the dean of the University of North Carolina at Chapel Hill
School of Law, working doggedly to try to convince the great
civil rights lawyer Julius Chambers to become the first director
of our Center for Civil Rights. He smiled and told me, "If we do
our work, the university and the state will close us down. This is
North Carolina. They aren't going to tolerate good lawyers representing Black and brown people."

It turned out that Chancellor Chambers was right. I was green.

Looking more broadly, as Princeton University's Eddie Glaude
Jr. put it, "At every moment in which our country stands on the
cusp of fundamental transformation, there are forces that double down on the ugliness." These forces insist, in one way or another, that "ours must remain a white nation in the vein of old
Europe." Professors Robert Korstad and Jim Leloudis have documented North Carolina's "one step forward" legacy in painful de-
tail, as have others. Phil Berger, former Speaker of the NC House
of Representatives Tim Moore, and NC Supreme Court Chief
Justice Paul Newby are part of a long and constantly reappear-
ing tradition. Perhaps we should stop saying, "This isn't North
Carolina."

Our forgetfulness is now augmented by the demand that our
children and our students not know what our racial history actually is. Bans on diversity, equity, and inclusion (DEI) measures
and critical race theory are pervasive. The very words are to be
stripped from our vocabulary. They are, like Voldemort's name,

never to be spoken. And North Carolina's story is to be white-washed clean. This is said to be necessary so that the children of white parents can remain psychologically joyous. No Wilmington, no Greensboro, no lynchings, no Pearsall Plan, no UNC slavery, no exclusion shall appear. Freedom has always been in the water in North Carolina. It is more important to keep white kids ignorantly buoyant than to face our brutal past. And surely, our children will be less concerned about nearly all-white governing Republican caucuses, about crushing racial disparities across every component of North Carolina life, about racial gerrymanders issued from the General Assembly, and about the tough discriminations of the criminal justice system if our racial history is suppressed. We seem to want kids to be even more clueless about our state's somber past than their parents are. As James Baldwin put it, we are "trapped in a history [we] do not understand, and until [we] understand, [we] cannot be released from it."

So, as citizens in North Carolina, we learn firsthand that, as John Kennedy put it, "Democracy is never a final achievement, it is a call to untiring effort." We, too, as philosopher Richard Rorty explained, are required to contribute our chapter, play our own part in "achieving our country." And, no doubt, our chapter is proving to be a rougher, more demanding road than we assumed it would be. It won't be full of easy valleys, lush hills, and welcoming pathways to new, unfolding liberties and generously expanded visions of equality. Instead, imposing burdens stand in our way. Old barriers and hatreds march against us. They have not, after all, disappeared. Maybe they never do.

Still, our tasks pale compared to those of many who have gone before us. We're not required to storm the beaches of Normandy, or be beaten to within an inch of our lives like Fannie Lou Hamer, or to face the hate-filled bullet like Dr. King. But we do have to make our mark now, or the cause of North Carolina will surely fail. And understandably, we didn't expect this to be our lot. Maybe people never do.

And the last fifteen years have shown that victories won't always readily come. Sometimes, we'll lose—and lose again. We'll discover that part of our charge, often the most essential part, is that we not lose heart. Getting up off the mat can be the engaged citizen's greatest attribute. I know that I struggle with it.

One of my good fortunes in North Carolina has been to have had famed professor and activist Dan Pollitt as a friend and mentor. He died fifteen years ago, and I miss him every week. Lots of people do. He was a veteran of a thousand battles in the cause of justice. Once, decades ago, I was scheduled to speak to a large ACLU gathering in Raleigh a few days after a particularly heartbreaking presidential election. Dan asked to go with me. I told him that I didn't know what to say to the distraught audience. What were we supposed to do?

Dan caught me up short in his kind way. "What do you mean, 'What are we supposed to do?'" he replied. "We dust ourselves off, gird up our loins, and get back in the fight." In fact, he added, "I'm going to find something for us to demonstrate against tomorrow, and we'll go down there just to keep in practice." It's obvious why I miss him. I'm pretty sure that a democracy that is

won, or re-won, can be even more fulfilling than a democracy
that is inherited.

## Citizen Engagement

This book concentrates on an ambitious suite of rights: rights to
equal political participation; rights to equal human dignity; as-
surances of judicial independence and integrity; rights of opportunity, both economic and educational; and rights to protect our
children and our planet on this day and into the future. It also
concentrates on ways to fix the ship that is North Carolina and
to more confidently, more constructively, and more generously
chart its course. On all these fronts, I obviously believe in the possibilities of institutions. Many changes that I advocate for could
not be achieved, in actuality, without successful legislative and
often judicial changes. Sometimes, I even press for constitutional
ratifications that no doubt require an altered, even much altered,
political landscape.

But none of these are possible in North Carolina without the
expansion of an obligation—not a right, but an obligation. It is a
duty, an undertaking, and a massive one; it is the heightened participation of engaged citizens. It is the marching feet, the joined
hands, the met minds, and the beating hearts of the much-moved
people of North Carolina. Political scientist Adam Bonica described the central, determinative factor in successfully opposing
movements of authoritarianism as, unsurprisingly, "whether people successfully mobilized" to contest them. That's not a great

mystery, of course. I love the way Bruce Springsteen (one of my leading constitutional sources) phrased it in his public attacks on the Trump administration in the early summer of 2025: "The last check on power after the checks and balances have failed is the people—you and me." Thus it is. Thus, I'm guessing, it should be. And that's true whether the checks and balances have merely failed or they've been purposefully broken down, decimated, as in North Carolina. Saving democracy is in our hands—joined ones.

And the broad mission is, as ever, the most central one: the belief that everyone counts and that all of us are full, first-class, fee simple members. When I was younger and did such things, I read Thurgood Marshall's oral argument in the re-hearing of *Brown v. Board of Education of Topeka*. Marshall used a phrase then that I've loved ever since: "These infant appellants are asserting the most important claim that can be set forth by children, the right to be treated as entire citizens of the society into which they have been born." *Entire citizens.* That's a notion worth keeping in your pocket.

I heard Ken Burns, the great documentarian, put it another way once: "You either believe all people are created equal or you don't—and if you do, things follow from that." And one of the things that follows is that you believe it without exception. There is no exclusion for "the unworthies." The notion of equal justice applies across the board. All means all.

That's not how things work in North Carolina right now. We're replete with exclusions, carve outs for Democrats, for

Black folks, for women, for LGBTQ+ people, for low-income and working-class Tar Heels, for kids in the wrong zip codes, and for those who aren't what we usually call evangelical Christians — those who are a step or two outside the traditionally empowered tribe and those who, in some way, have been offered something other than full dignity and full membership, something more like the back of the hand.

## The Stakes Revealed

In this battle, I concede that we Democrats haven't always behaved as if we understand the peril that we face. We haven't wanted to name the extremism, or frankly, the sedition of our opponents. We haven't seemed to comprehend that rejecting democracy, trying to defeat it, is literally rejecting the United States and our defining mission. It is casting aside our meaning as a people and committing sedition against what Lincoln described as our "leading object as a nation," the principle of "liberty to all."

If you are in an existential struggle for your state and your nation, then you don't behave the way we often have here. If someone acts to take away your form of government, your rights of equal participation, and your sense of human dignity, you stop worrying about whether you might piss them off if you speak up or that you won't be able to find some longed-for common ground in a purported bargaining process. If somebody shows you repeatedly that they mean to destroy the values that are most central to your existence, you don't say, "No worries, friend, maybe I can meet you halfway." A big part of why North Carolina Republicans have been able to successfully govern through perjury is that North Carolina Democrats have too often let them. As Frederick Douglass tried to teach us, sometimes "it is not the light that is needed, but the fire, not the gentle shower, but the thunder."

But it is on this front—and I can't believe that I am writing this—this crucial front of determined engagement that President Donald Trump, Judge Jackson Griffin, Paul Newby, Phil Berger, and the like have delivered a gift. They have, finally, gone public. They have displayed unadorned their lust for autocracy, their disdain for constitutional democracy, their antipathy to "liberty and justice for all." If we had thought that they wouldn't actually carry out their destructive mission, or if we had assumed that they might just step up to the line and then remember what we were all taught in grade school, then we were wrong: 2025 was the year of crossing the Rubicon.

There is no need to rehearse Trump's fulsome transgressions, but he has not sought to be dictator only for a day, as he had boasted initially, but to assume the mantle permanently. He has moved to control every aspect of US life—public, private, political, economic, social, civic, educational, journalistic, legal, and spiritual—through a regime of terror, extortion, and corruption that is literally totalitarian. The cat is fully out of the bag. And Republicans, including Republican leaders in North Carolina, have either cheered him on or been so terrified to face the famed Trumpian wrath that they have wallowed in submission. Forgetting, as Kennedy explained in his magnificent inaugural address that those "who foolishly sought power by riding the back of the tiger ended up inside."

And in North Carolina, where the democracy-ending work has been more covert, more civil, and less obviously wrapped in cruelty, violence, and criminality, the brutal door has been thrown undeniably and permanently open as well. Every Tar Heel has been made to stare it in the face. The Republican General Assembly has repeatedly mocked the electorate by comically removing the constitutional powers of the governor and other statewide elected officials whenever the winning candidate is a Democrat. Council of State races cannot be gerrymandered, and when Republicans lose these races (as they usually do), the lawmakers shuffle the deck, transferring powers to any absurd character so long as they are a Republican and not actually the person who was assigned to do the duty. They seem to think that the charade is funny, like putting the librarian in charge of the state militia. But North Carolinians don't. We think that we vote for something, not just an empty title, when we elect a governor. And we don't expect the assignments to disappear if Senator Berger doesn't get the winner he wants. Now, in truth, in any other state in America, such a result would be invalidated by the state supreme court. But in North Carolina, there is no state supreme court.

And now, North Carolina's Republican justices have notoriously upped the ante. In the Judge Griffin case, they used all their official powers to try to literally steal an election—not as a thief in the night, just as a thief, walking into the house at midday, taking the treasure and then bragging about it. This stunned the nation and outraged North Carolinians in ways that I have never seen them angered before. No law was cited, and no attempt at justification was rendered. They simply offered the middle finger to Tar Heel voters and said, *What are you going to do about it? We're the ones in the black robes, and we're Republicans, and we're used to lying about what we're doing. We're in the business of crushing democracy in favor of Republican power. That's our shared agenda. And now we find that, in order to crush democracy, we're forced to steal an election outright. So, get used to it.*

I'm not saying what justices Paul Newby, Philip Berger Jr., Tamara Barringer, and Trey Allen did was criminal. But I have no doubt that what they did was decidedly more destructive than what Leslie McCrae Dowless managed in eastern North Carolina in 2018. It's true, of course, that the federal courts eventually stopped them. But they acted finally, fully, completely, knowingly, and illegally to complete the stickup. And everyone in North Carolina knows it.

So, our politics have changed. As they should. These four justices should, of course, be drummed out of the North Carolina court system through the ballot box. As I'm sure they will be. But it's not just the justices. The North Carolina Republican Party was itself central to the effort, constantly singing Judge Griffin's praises and pressing his cause. I know less than nothing about the internal deliberations of North Carolina Republicans. I'm not on the guest list. But I can't imagine that justices Newby and Berger decided to pull the plug on North Carolina's democracy without the permission of the kingpins. It's too big a step, not one for the lickspittle alone.

We learned something else from the Judge Griffin adventure as well. While he moved to steal a state supreme court seat, and North Carolina Republican judges waved him through the door, North Carolina citizens erupted. From every county, every court-house square, every street corner, every main street, and every bustling downtown in the state, Tar Heels said, loudly and heat-edly, that they wouldn't stand for it. I'll confess to being in some of those agitated places myself, among such riled-up people. And I can report that the explosion was not limited to the usual cast of characters. They were Republicans, Democrats, independents, and otherwise typically uninterested people. They were young, old, and in-between. They were every shade of the spectrum. They were raging grannies and their grandkids, amazed by their elders' language. And, of course, there were veterans—lots of vet-erans. Apparently, people don't like fighting for their country and then having their votes taken away, even if the guy trying to can-cel your vote is wearing a Confederate uniform. Who knew?

Lots of regular folks don't like getting involved in politics or going to boisterous demonstrations. They have lives to lead, kids to raise, jobs (often more than one) to see to, and kin to care for. And regular folks aren't inclined to believe that politicians whom they might have heard of for years really are out to end Ameri-can democracy, especially if they wear flag pins on their lapels, go to Baptist churches on Sunday mornings, and are regulars at the Rotary Club. But Tar Heels aren't willing to have their faces rubbed in it either. *I wasn't willing to believe that you were trying to decimate constitutional democracy,* they seemed to say, *but then you stole an election right before my eyes. I won't put up with that.*

And a lot of people who have prospered far more dramatically than "regular folks" in North Carolina, and who have assumed that they would be left unbothered in their comfort and blessings, now must see that their way of life, their prosperity, their patriotism and their endless pledges of allegiance, their avowed belief in the Sermon on the Mount, their pride in a history of idealism and promise, and their commitment to the marvels of the American Dream are now, literally and undeniably, on the line.

One way of seeing this is that North Carolina Republicans overplayed their hand in 2025. Another is that there's a limit to villainy—even for its most consistent practitioners.

I know that some will consider the comparison overblown. But in 1861, Ulysses S. Grant said, "There are but two political parties now, patriots and traitors." It's tough, and it's unfortunate. But it's accurate. That's what we have in North Carolina now, today, "patriots and traitors." This is also, therefore, the most important fight that we've faced in the Tar Heel State in a half-century. It's on everyone's shoulders.

## ACKNOWLEDGMENTS

I'm very grateful to Lynn York of Blair, not only for getting this book to the light of day, but for suggesting the project in the first place. The Blair folks are, as always, great to work with. Taylor Bello did a remarkable job of editing. As I mentioned in the text, I'm grateful for Patrick Bradey's coauthorship of chapter 8. I also strongly appreciate the terrific research efforts of Hannah Litty, particularly on the education chapter. David Neal of the Southern Environmental Law Center was immensely helpful in the climate-change discussion, as was Yevonne Brannon, of Public Schools First NC, in the *Leandro* and school-voucher sections. I appreciate both Yevonne's and David's careful reads. All of my work benefits from the assistance of my friend Tyla Olson. And, as ever, I'm grateful for the inspiration of the committed activists whom I work with every day across the Tar Heel State.

## BIBLIOGRAPHY
## PARTIAL LIST OF SOURCES

An Act to Reenact the Child Tax Credit. S. 641, 157th N.C. General Assembly (2025).

An Act to Study and Modify Certain Coastal Management Policies. H.R. 819, 150th N.C. General Assembly (2011).

Andersen, Kurt. *Evil Geniuses: The Unmaking of America: A Recent History.* Random House, 2020.

Article I, Section 22 | The Right to Reproductive Freedom with Protections for Health and Safety. Article I, Ohio Constitution (2023).

Ashby, Warren. *Frank Porter Graham: A Southern Liberal.* John F. Blair, 1980.

Bajpai, Avi. "A Near-Total Abortion Ban Proposed in NC Won't Be Taken Up, House Speaker Says." *Raleigh News & Observer,* April 8, 2025.

"Ballot Tracker: Outcome of Abortion-Related State Constitutional Amendment Measures in the 2024 Election." KFF. https://www.kff.org/womens-health-policy/dashboard/ballot-tracker-status-of-abortion-related-state-constitutional-amendment-measures/.

Barnett, Ned. "As NC Legislators Swerve to Extremes, Bring Back the Guardrails." *Raleigh News & Observer,* December 1, 2024,

quoting Ran Coble. https://newsobserver.com/opinion/article
296338909.html.

Barnett, Ned. "There's a Bill to Restore Fairness to NC Elections,
But It's Locked Away." *Raleigh News & Observer*, February 3,
2025.

Berman, Ari. *Minority Rule: The Right-Wing Attack on the Will
of the People—and the Fight to Resist It.* Farrar, Straus and Gir-
oux, 2024.

Bonner, Lynn. "NC Legislature Overrides Governor's Veto of
Abortion Ban to Make New Restrictions Law." *NC Newsline*,
May 16, 2023.

Bonner, Lynn. "NC Supreme Court Orders RFK Jr.'s Name Removed, Counties to Reprint Millions of Ballots." *NC Newsline*,
September 10, 2024. https://ncnewsline.com/briefs/nc
-supreme-court-orders-rfk-jr-s-name-removed-counties-to
-reprint-millions-of-ballots/.

Boughton, Melissa. "NC Republicans Double Down on Partisan
Gerrymandering Ahead of Tomorrow's Supreme Court Arguments." *NC Newsline*, March 25, 2019, quoting Michael Li.

Brownstein, Ronald. "Why Republican Voter Restrictions Are a
Race Against Time." *CNN*, March 23, 2021.

Bruni, Frank. "Republicans in North Carolina Are Treading a
Terrifying Path." *New York Times*, January 16, 2025.

Coastal Conservation Association v. State of N.C. 285 N.C. App.
267 (2022).

Common Cause v. Rucho. 318 F. Supp. 3d 777 (M.D.N.C. 2018),
vacated 139 S. Ct. 2484 (2019).

Covington v. North Carolina. 270 F. Supp. 3d at 881 (2017).

Bibliography

149

Covington v. North Carolina. 316 F.R.D. 117, 124 (M.D.N.C. 2016), affirmed 137 S. Ct. 2211 (2017).
Crowell, Michael. *History of North Carolina Judicial Elections.*
University of North Carolina School of Government, 2020.
"DEI Legislation Tracker." *Chronicle of Higher Education.*
https://www.chronicle.com/article/here-are-the-states-where
-lawmakers-are-seeking-to-ban-colleges-dei-efforts.
Dobbs v. Jackson Women's Health Organization. 597 U.S. 215
(2022).
Eanes, Zachery, and Emily Peck. "North Carolina Has More Low-
Wage Workers than National Average." *Axios Raleigh*, August
12, 2024. https://www.axios.com/local/raleigh/2024/08/12
/north-carolina-low-wage-workers-national-average-minimum
-wage.
Editorial. "Transgender Law Makes North Carolina Pioneer in
Bigotry." *New York Times*, March 25, 2016.
Energy Security and Affordability Act. S. 261, 157th N.C. General
Assembly (2025).
*Federalist Papers*, no. 47 (James Madison).
Fields, Aryn. "Federal Judge Blocks Trump Administration's
Transgender Military Service Ban." *Human Rights Campaign*,
March 27, 2025. https://www.hrc.org/press-releases/federal
-judge-blocks-trump-administrations-transgender-military
-service-ban.
Fletcher, Michael A. "In North Carolina, Unimpeded GOP
Drives State Hard to the Right." *Washington Post*, May 25, 2013.
Foner, Eric. *The Second Founding: How the Civil War and Recon-
struction Remade the Constitution.* W.W. Norton, 2019.

Guinassi, Luciana Perez Uribe. "Raleigh Protesters Vow to Stand
as 'United Working Class' Against Trump Policies." *Raleigh
News & Observer*, May 1, 2025. https://www.newsobserver
.com/news/politics-government/article305491366.html#story
link=cpyat.

Harper v. Hall. 384 N.C. 326–345 (2022), vacated 868 S.E. 2d 418
(2023).

Hawes, Jennifer Berry, and Mollie Simon. "Segregation Academies across the South Are Getting Millions in Taxpayer Dollars." *ProPublica*, November 18, 2024.

Hazen, Rick. "Divided Three Judge Court Holds North Carolina
Congressional Redistricting an Unconstitutional Partisan Gerrymander, Considers New Districts for 2018 Elections." *Election Law Blog*, August 27, 2018.

Henkel, Clayton. "'Maybe the Cruelty Is the Point': NC Lawmakers Ban Gender-Affirming Care for Transgender Minors
Following Tense Floor Debate." *NC Newsline*, June 29, 2023.
https://ncnewsline.com/briefs/maybe-the-cruelty-is-the-point
-nc-lawmakers-ban-gender-affirming-care-for-transgender
-minors-following-tense-floor-debate/.

Hoke County Board of Education v. State of North Carolina.
2022-NCSC-108 (2022).

Horowitch, Rose, and Zoë Richards. "North Carolina Republicans Override Democratic Governor's Veto of 12-Week Abortion Ban." *NBC News*, May 16, 2023. https://www.nbcnews
.com/politics/politics-news/north-carolina-republicans-aim
-override-governors-abortion-ban-veto-rcna84651.

"How Climate Change Makes Hurricanes More Destructive." Environmental Defense Fund. https://www.edf.org/climate /how-climate-change-makes-hurricanes-more-destructive.

*Hurricane Helene Recovery.* North Carolina Office of State Budget and Management, 2024. https://www.osbm.nc.gov /hurricane-helene-dna/open.

Ingram, Kyle. "Federal Lawsuit Accusing NC Senate Districts of Diluting Black Votes Set to Go to Trial." *Raleigh News & Observer*, February 3, 2025.

Johnson, Lyndon. "The American Promise." Washington, DC, March 15, 1965.

King, Martin Luther, Jr. "I Have a Dream," Washington, DC, August 28, 1963.

Kingdollar, Brandon. "North Carolina Senate Proposal Again Seeks to Bar Transgender People from Specified Public Restrooms." *NC Newsline*, March 27, 2025. https://ncnewsline.com /2025/03/27/north-carolina-senate-proposal-again-seeks-to -bar-transgender-people-from-specified-public-restrooms/.

Leandro v. State. 346 N.C. 336 (1997).

Leloudis, James L., and Robert Korstad. *Fragile Democracy: The Struggle over Race and Voting Rights in North Carolina.* The University of North Carolina Press, 2020.

MacKinnon, J. B. "True Grit." *The Atavist Magazine*, no. 132, October 2022. https://magazine.atavist.com/true-grit-cows -core-banks-hurricane-dorian-survival/.

Malcolm, Scott, Elizabeth Marshall, Marcel Aillery, Paul Heisey, Michael Livingston, and Kelly Day-Rubenstein. *Agricultural*

*Adaptation to a Changing Climate.* (United States Department of Agriculture Economic Research Service, 2012), Report no. 136.

Manning, Howard. Memorandum of Decision. March 26, 2001.

Marr, Chuck, Chye-Ching Huang, Arloc Sherman, and Brandon DeBot. "EITC and Child Tax Credit Promote Work, Reduce Poverty, and Support Children's Development, Research Finds." *Center on Budget and Policy Priorities,* October 1, 2015. https://www.cbpp.org/research/eitc-and-child-tax-credit-promote-work-reduce-poverty-and-support-childrens-development.

Masten, Paige. "A Harsh New Abortion Ban Won't Pass in NC, But You Still Should Be Alarmed." *Raleigh News & Observer,* April 9, 2025. https://www.newsobserver.com/opinion/article303832906.html#storylink=cpy.

*NC School Vouchers: Using Tax Dollars to Discriminate Against Students & Families.* Public Schools First NC, 2024. https://publicschoolsfirstnc.org/wp-content/uploads/2024/02/1.2024_Voucher-Report-Jan-2024-Compressed.pdf.

"NC Teacher Pay Now Ranks 43rd." *Public Ed Works,* May 1, 2025. https://publicedworks.org/2025/05/nc-teacher-pay-now-ranks-43rd/.

"No. 1 in Business, No. 38 in Teacher Pay." *Public Ed Works,* May 8, 2024.

Nonpartisan Redistricting Process. H.R. 606, 151st N.C. General Assembly (2013).

*North Carolina Climate Risk Assessment and Resilience Plan.* North Carolina Department of Environmental Quality, 2020.

https://files.nc.gov/ncdeq/climate-change/resilience-plan
/2020-Climate-Risk-Assessment-and-Resilience-Plan.pdf.

Obergefell v. Hodges. 135 S. Ct. 2071 (2015).

"Offshore Wind Development." North Carolina Department of
Environmental Quality. https://www.deq.nc.gov/energy
-climate/offshore-wind-development.

Planned Parenthood of Southeastern Pennsylvania v. Casey. 505
U.S. 833 (1992).

Power Bill Reduction Act, The. S. 266, 157th N.C. General Assembly (2025). https://www.ncleg.gov/Sessions/2025/Bills
/Senate/PDF/S266v4.pdf.

Protect Women's Healthcare. S. 909, 156th N.C. General Assembly (2024).

Public Schools First NC, accessed March 1, 2025. www.public
schoolsfirstnc.org.

"Refundable Child Tax Credit." *NC Budget & Tax Center,* April
2025. https://ncbudget.org/ctcfactsheet/.

Research Staff. "A Tale of Two Caucuses." *Carolina Forward*, January 21, 2025.

Richardson, Heather Cox. "January 12, 2025." *Letters from an
American*, January 12, 2025. https://heathercoxrichardson
.substack.com/p/january-12-2025.

Robert F. Kennedy Jr. v. North Carolina State Board of Elections.
https://appellate.nccourts.org/orders.php?t=P&court=1&id
=439795&pdf=1&a=0&docket=1&dev=1 (ballot access/
removal).

Rorty, Richard. *Achieving Our Country: Leftist Thought in
Twentieth-Century America*. Harvard University Press, 1970.

154 Bibliography

Rucho v. Common Cause. 588 U.S. 684 (2019).

Schlemmer, Liz. "NC Again Ranks near Bottom for Effort to Fund Public Schools." *WUNC*, December 13, 2024. https://www.wunc.org/education/2024-12-13/nc-ranks-49-school-funding-effort-education-law-center-making-the-grade.

Sirota, Alexandra. "State Budget Agreement Doubles Down Once More on Regressive Tax Policies." *NC Newsline*, June 29, 2016.

Stein v. Berger, et al. No. 114PO25 (May 2025). (Justice Earls, dissenting.)

Stern, Mark Joseph. "North Carolina Passes Law Allowing Magistrates to Refuse to Marry Same-Sex Couples." *Slate*, June 11, 2015.

Stern, Mark Joseph. "North Carolina Republicans' Legislative Coup Is an Attack on Democracy." *Slate*, December 15, 2016.

Students for Fair Admissions, Inc. v. President and Fellows of Harvard College. 600 U.S. 101 (2023).

Sullivan, Caroline. "The North Carolina Supreme Court's Three-Part Attack on Democracy." *Democracy Docket*, May 2, 2023. https://www.democracydocket.com/analysis/the-north-carolina-supreme-courts-three-part-attack-on-democracy/.

Text of Proposed Amendment, Amending Article II, Constitution of Arizona, relating to the fundamental right to abortion. September 12, 2023.

Thompson, Caitlin. "North Carolina's Notorious Climate Change Law—The Rich Are Ok, the Poor Aren't." *Coda*, June 29, 2021. https://www.codastory.com/climate-crisis/climate-change-north-carolina/.

Thucydides. *The History of the Peloponnesian War*. Trans. Richard
    Crawley. Project Gutenberg, 2003. https://www.gutenberg
    .org/files/7142/7142-h/7142-h.htm.
Town of Carrboro v. Duke Energy Corporation. 24CV003385-670
    Orange County Superior Court (2024). https://climatecase
    chart.com/wp-content/uploads/case-documents/2024
    /20241204_docket-24CV003385-670_complaint.pdf.
Wan, William. "Inside the Republican Creation of the North
    Carolina Voting Bill Dubbed the 'Monster' Law." *Washington
    Post*, September 2, 2016. https://www.washingtonpost.com
    /politics/courts_law/inside-the-republican-creation-of-the
    -north-carolina-voting-bill-dubbed-the-monster-law/2016/09
    /01/79162398-6adf-11e6-8225-fbb8a6fc65bc_story.html.
Zhu, Christine. "Stein Calls on Congress to Preserve Electric Ve-
    hicle Industry Tax Credits in Raleigh Speech." *NC Newsline*,
    May 28, 2025. https://ncnewsline.com/briefs/stein-calls-on
    -congress-to-preserve-electric-vehicle-industry-tax-credits-in
    -raleigh-speech/.